LITTLE ENGLISH BACKYARDS

Roddy Llewellyn

Salem House
Salem, New Hampshire

To Tania

First published in the United States
by Salem House, 1985. A member of the
Merrimack Publishers' Circle, 47 Pelham Road,
Salem NH 03079.

House editor Denis Ingram
Designed by Bob Swan

Text set in Plantin Light
by Advanced Filmsetters (Glasgow) Ltd

Printed and bound in Italy by Mondadori

ISBN 0-88162-072-6

CONTENTS

	Acknowledgements	6
	Preface	7
1	The wild backyard	9
2	The landscaped backyard	29
3	Trompe l'oeil backyards	49
4	Focal point backyards	61
5	Terraced backyards	69
6	Very small backyards	75
7	Features	83
	Appendix I. Plant lists	89
	Appendix II. The beautiful backyard – the D.I.Y. way	94
	Index	95

AUTHOR'S ACKNOWLEDGEMENTS

The compiling of this book was made all the more enjoyable by the many kind people who allowed me to include their backyards. These include John Codrington, John Junner, Roy Alderson, Colin Wells-Brown, H. H. The Raj Mata of Jaipur, Zandra Rhodes, The Countess of Westmorland, David Holmes, Viscountess Hardinge, Mr and Mrs Martin Summers, Norma Heyman, Jane Egerton-Warburton, Colin Weston, Mark Hudson, Mr and Mrs Maurice FitzGibbon, Mr and Mrs Michael Bradley, Ron Kitaj, Mrs Cassell, Mr and Mrs Harry Conlin, Mr and Mrs Bruce Dowling, Brian Cox, Robin Miller, Madame Ginette Spanier and Myles Challis.

I am very grateful to Mrs Cross and Alan Gloak of the London Garden Society and very special thanks to Pamela Bullmore who helped me with the many gardens she designed. I would also like to thank Tor van Moyland, Alan Sawyer, Robin Williams, Tim Plant, Meredith Pilcher, Patrick O'Callaghan, Christopher Williams, Randall Siddeley, Nick Dickinson, Mike Bell, Leonardo Pieroni, Mrs Sainty, Paul Temple, Karen Kaliszewski, Mark and Marigold Kingston, John and Sarah Standing, Gillian Lynne and Peter Land for their help in so many different ways.

Finally, although officially recorded as a 'dropout' in Robert Lacey's *Majesty*, I am grateful to him for permitting his garden to be included in the book and for allowing me to drop in!

R.Ll.

PUBLISHER'S ACKNOWLEDGEMENTS

The publishers gratefully acknowledge the following persons for granting permission for reproduction of the colour photographs: Behram Kapadia (p. 14) and Neil Holmes (p. 73). All other photographs were taken by Hugh Palmer.

The line drawings of garden plans are by Robin Williams and the plant identification drawings are by Nils Solberg. (The camera symbol* on the line drawings indicates the position of the photographer.)

The quotation in the heading on p. 62 is from the *Kubla Khan*, by Samuel Taylor Coleridge (1772–1834).

*

PUBLISHER'S NOTE

Readers are requested to note that in order to make the text intelligible in both hemispheres, plant flowering times, etc. are described in terms of seasons, not months. The following table provides an approximate 'translation' of seasons into months for the two hemispheres.

NORTHERN HEMISPHERE		SOUTHERN HEMISPHERE	NORTHERN HEMISPHERE		SOUTHERN HEMISPHERE
Mid-winter	= January	= Mid-summer	Mid-summer	= July	= Mid-winter
Late winter	= February	= Late summer	Late summer	= August	= Late winter
Early spring	= March	= Early autumn	Early autumn	= September	= Early spring
Mid-spring	= April	= Mid-autumn	Mid-autumn	= October	= Mid-spring
Late spring	= May	= Late autumn	Late autumn	= November	= Late spring
Early summer	= June	= Early winter	Early winter	= December	= Early summer

PREFACE

The population explosion may explain why so many of us have been crammed into smaller and smaller spaces. The pulse of the economy throbs in cities which is why most of us have to live in them. Well, let's make the best of it and convert the little space allowed as best we can! Our ancestors were used to having uninterrupted rolling acres, later generations had 'gardens', and the present generation, squeezed into less space than ever before has to do with a backyard. I trust that the contents of this book will fulfil the inherent desire of most urban dwellers to be closer to Mother Nature, as well as an inspiration to improve their plots.

The derivation of the word 'yard' comes from the old English 'geard', meaning fence or enclosure. A present day backyard conjures up an image of a concreted area in cooler parts of the world, and a dusty one in warmer climes. The intention of this book is to remedy such sites and transform them into your own little paradise. Although all suggested concepts of design are universal, the plants which appear in the book were all found in London gardens. Sadly, owing to constraints on time and budget, research was confined to this city only.

Soil, climate and temperature vary so tremendously according to altitude, proximity to the sea, and for many other reasons. By all means, try out the plants you see included in this book. If they do not like your particular backyard, it is always worth having a good look at the gardens of your more imaginative gardening neighbours and copying their example. As you will see, several of the photographs have a key to facilitate plant identification.

If you do not intend to build your backyard yourself, it is sensible to invite at least three gardening contractors on a tender basis, and assess their prices and characters alike. If they have a portfolio, all the better. The majority of backyards which feature in this book have been designed and built professionally. Incidentally, the reason why my present garden is not featured in the book is simply because at the time of writing I have just moved house and the new garden has yet to be made presentable.

I had enormous fun writing this book and I hope that some of my enjoyment rubs off on you, the reader.

R.Ll.

A writer's garden (p. 10). This is the first of four areas created
from a long, thin garden. Behind it is dense planting so that none of
the rest of the garden is visible. However, a path leading through
it proves irresistible to the visitor . . .(*continued* p. 10)

I

THE WILD BACKYARD

The wild garden has the enormous advantage of needing very little maintenance and in particular, it is an ideal solution for someone who travels a lot. The plants, both invited and uninvited, are allowed to grow pretty well as they wish, and are only reduced in size if they become too invasive or start to choke other wanted plants. Such an area is always relaxing: it is as if the plants' feeling of safety is instilled into the human visitor.

Ground cover plants (pp. 22 and 90) play a very important part in this style of gardening as they act as weed-suppressors. They are planted as soon as the ground has been cleared of unwanted perennial weeds.

It is especially enchanting to find such an area in the middle of a city as it lends a strong feeling of tranquil countryside. It is also a place where wild life feels safe – birds can be encouraged to nest in strategically placed nesting boxes and a clump of common stinging-nettles can be established in one corner out of the way to invite many of our indigenous butterflies to breed there.

If you are in favour of this style, far less careful planning is required than usual. Apart from the actual planting programme, most thought should be given to the positioning of paths alongside which a few special eye-catching plants should be included. Many suitable plants can be found growing on derelict sites and others you may be lucky enough to receive as gifts from friends who live in the country. Removal of such plants from their natural habitat must of course be undertaken with utmost discretion. The wild garden, therefore, is cheap to run without the need for bedding and other nursery plants. There is seldom any need to consult your gardening books to find out what you should be doing now!

Parts of larger gardens, which have become too much work, can always be treated in this way. They can be made accessible along mown paths connected to the lawn, to facilitate mowing.

Finally, plan a spot for a bench. There you can sit, away from all the pressures of life, and allow Mother Nature to caress your brow.

A writer's garden

LOCATION: *North London*

These two gardens are part of a long, thin area which measures 40 × 125 ft (12 × 37.5 m). It has been divided up into four, each part having been laid out in such a way as to have a different feel about it. By dividing up long, thin gardens in this way, an extra feeling of space is created, especially if each section is not immediately visible from the other.

The part of the garden you walk into from the house is dominated by an informal pond. As with the other 'gardens within a garden', it has delightful informal feeling about it. The large camellia behind the pond is 'Contessa Lavinia Maggi'. Around the water's edge is planted an assortment of water-loving plants, namely three ligularias, including *L. clivorum* 'Desdemona'; the sensitive fern *(Onoclea sensibilis)*; the royal fern *(Osmunda regalis)*; *Lysichitum americanum*

(continued from p. 8) . . . who, having walked through the thickly planted second section, is greeted by a delightful, York-paved area bursting with scented roses, lilies and a host of other plants which give the feeling of a cottage garden.

Robinia frisia pseudocacia

Rosemary with Clematis 'Rouge Cardinale'

Rose 'Bloomfield Abundance'

Rose 'Bobbie James'

Hebe 'Blue Clouds'

Clematis 'Etoile Violette'

Veronica perfoliata

Euphorbia characias wulfenii

Ceanothus 'Burkwoodii'

Astrantia major

Papaver somnifera

Lilium 'Pink Tiger'

Alchemilla mollis

Lilium 'Burgundy'

and the unnamed *Lysichitum* hybrid–cross between *americanum* and *camtschatcensis*–with white flowers and glaucous leaves, infinitely more exciting than the familiar 'Golden Skunk Cabbage'. A *Gunnera manicata* has remained small, probably through not being protected in the winter. In the pond itself is water hawthorn*(Aponogeton distachyus)*, one of the very few water plants which will flower in dense shade.

Around the paved area are the single white camellia 'Francis Hanger' in a pot, protected by *Prunus subhirtella* 'Autumnalis Rosea', the indispensable, pink winter-flowering cherry; *Trachystemon orientale*, flowering in late winter/early spring, vast-leaved and flourishing in dry shade; *Dicentra* 'Langtrees' with blue leaves and white flowers which appear for most of the summer; *Rhododendron yakushimanum*; the winter-flowering honeysuckle *(Lonicera fragrantissima)*; *Acanthus mollis*; and *Teucrium fruticans* (needs protection in the winter).

A path lures the visitor on further, through a woodland section which is mainly planted up with spectacular foliage plants. It is so thickly planted that it feels like a leafy tunnel.

Out into the open once more to the third section of the garden, which is chiefly paved with York stone. Plants such as *Alchemilla mollis, Erigeron macranthus, Viola, Sedum, Helianthemum*, single *Campanula* species as well as *Chrysanthemum* 'White Bonnet', are allowed to grow haphazardly between the paving stones.

The planting all around is informal and everything is left to its own devices unless serious strangulation is threatened. There are roses everywhere. They include 'Louise Odier', 'Penelope', 'Iceberg', 'Bloomfield Abundance', 'Mousseline', 'Little White Pet', 'Frühlingsgold', 'Bobbie James', 'Etoile de Hollande', 'Perle d'Or', and 'Plentiful'.

There are many varieties of clematis, including 'Etoile Violette', 'Miss Bateman', 'Rouge Cardinale' (growing up the rosemary and up the silver birch). Other plants to be found here are: *Erica arborea*; *Agapanthus umbellatus*; an assortment of lilies in pots and in the ground (succeeding better in the former); *Nerine bowdenii*; *Ceratostigma willmottianum*; *Rheum palmatum*; geraniums in variety, notably the little used *G. phaeum*, with almost black flowers in late spring/early summer; *Fuschia* spp.; *Mahonia bealei*; *Ceanothus* 'Burkwoodii'; the hardy hebe 'Blue Clouds', which flowers twice a season and oblingingly turns plum-purple during the winter; camellias 'Donation' and 'Guilio Nuccio'; *Viburnum davidii* frames the steps and *Robinia pseudoacacia* 'Frisia' and *Magnolia grandiflora* 'Exmouth' supply privacy from neighbouring gardens.

This garden was made from a rubbish dump. Tons of spent hops and manure were incorporated into it (the soil was described by an early visitor as 'grey face powder').

The philosophy of this garden's creator is:

1 Split up space to create mystery. Turn corners and vary levels.
2 Use evergreens as 'bones': these provide interest all the year through.
3 Rely on foliage form more than flowers.
4 Always have something in bloom with as many dramatic foliage plants as possible.
5 *Always* have water, even a sink or 'dribble'; it's life.
6 Create an overall effect of calming green to rest visitors from the street.

One of the author's previous gardens

LOCATION: *Fulham*

This is a yard which has been made to look very much larger than it really is by means of clever planting. It contains many evergreens which give it all-year-round interest. There are two sitting-out areas, one immediately outside the French windows, and the other near to the back of the garden. Access to the back is by means of two winding paths consisting of concrete-moulded paving stones of various sizes. This same material is used for the further paved area, none of it being laid on foundations but merely placed straight onto Mother Earth. This is no accident – the paths can easily be moved.

The view from the French window of this basement flat consists of verdant, almost jungle-like planting, with various plants specially chosen to 'do a particular job'. The *Yucca gloriosa*, for instance, was planted in the foreground to catch the eye, which in turn is led towards the bay pillar and then onto the plants and other features at the back, thus luring the visitor further into the yard. The massive rosemary pillar did not find itself there just by chance either. It not only 'blocks off' the bench from view of the flat, but also hides a rhododendron which can be seen from the window, but only via a large mirror on the right-hand wall.

The bench at the end of the garden is positioned in such a way as to command the best open view. It looks out straight onto a large expanse of sky with a huge tree in the distance, and neither the house itself or the modern building opposite in view. To enhance the 'enclosed' feeling it is surrounded by an arbor over which evergreen honeysuckle and *Clematis × jackmanii* are allowed to scramble.

Ten years ago, this space consisted of nothing but paving with the occasional gap containing a dead shrub. The only other sign of life was a large, diseased sycamore in the far corner—a wholly unsuitable tree for a small yard. *Acer pseudoplatanus* is too large, has no ornamental features and scatters its seeds far too prolifically. Once this tree had been removed the stump had to be killed. Unless the actual stump is treated, it can produce healthy new shoots, which eventually form an ugly thicket.

Back to the garden itself. I lost no time and planted two rhododendrons either side of a maiden hair tree, *Ginkgo biloba* and, up against the wall which was north-facing, a magnolia *M. grandiflora* 'Exmouth'. I am a

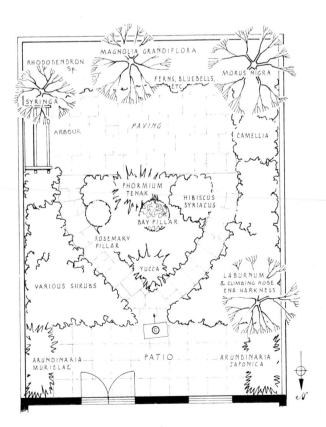

The author in one of his earlier gardens. The 'jungle' effect has
been achieved with evergreen plants with distinctive and varying
foliage. As a result, this garden can be enjoyed all the year round,
as it looks much the same during the winter.

great believer in 'posterity' planting and so I tucked a black mulberry *(Morus nigra)* in the other corner. The sycamore tree stump was camouflaged with a variegated ivy *(Hedera helix* 'Goldheart'). The carpet for this higher planting included drifts of bluebells, ferns, *Tiarella cordifolia* (foam flower), *Vinca minor* (lesser periwinkle), a group of lily of the valley *(Convallaria)* in the darkest corner under the mulberry. Many spring bulbs were also included here as well as self-seeding fox-gloves and non-white flowering opium poppies *(Papaver somniferum)*. This array of plants meant that the end patch was always interesting and full of colour. In mild winters, the ferns maintained their garb and added interest to the garden, along with their evergreen neighbours.

Further into the garden were included plants and shrubs chosen for their colour. A red camellia 'Adolphe Audusson' was planted against the west wall with a variegated dogwood *(Cornus alba* 'Sibirica') to keep it company. In between the two was

planted a white jasmine *(Jasminum officinale)* to cover quickly the trellis above the wall.

The centre of the yard is dominated by a bay pillar. This is surrounded by an established clump of *Phormium tenax* (New Zealand flax), the hardiest palm of all *Trachycarpus fortunei* (otherwise known as the Chusan or windmill palm), and several herbaceous plants, including *Paeonia* 'Sarah Bernhardt' (apple-blossom pink), the yellow *Iris* 'Desert Song', macleaya and three hostas: *H. sieboldiana, H.* 'Thomas Hogg' and *H. fortunei* 'Aureo-marginata'.

The sitting-out area immediately next to the house contains various plants. On one side, there is a climbing rose 'Ena Harkness', specially chosen to be trained up the laburnum. They flower at the same time and the mixture of red and yellow makes all the neighbours sit up! Along side this rose was a bamboo *(Arundinaria japonica)*. This was chosen for the noise its leaves make in the wind – a lovely rustling. Correspondingly, another bamboo *(A. murieliae)* was planted on the other side for the same reason, as well as for its beautiful feathery foliage which arch down to the ground. Here, there was also a passion flower *(Passiflora caerulea)* trained over the French windows along with the semi-evergreen 'Mermaid' rose. The passion flower is cut back severely every year in the autumn and the end result is a curtain of flower throughout the summer. Against the house itself, was planted a wisteria which helped to camouflage an ugly down-pipe, and at its base there was a healthy clump of white tobacco whose strong scent wafts straight into the sitting room on balmy summer evenings. The tobacco plant is usually treated as an annual but, owing to the microclimate of London, this plant carried on flowering for four seasons until it was knocked over the head in the very severe winter of 1981/1982. So busy and varied is the planting here that no-one believes it is only 40×17 ft (12×5 m)!

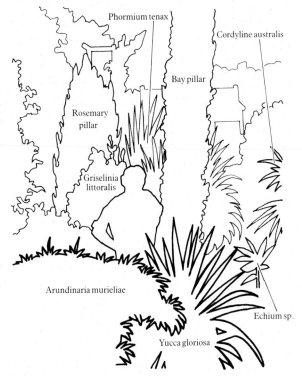

Phormium tenax

Cordyline australis

Bay pillar

Rosemary pillar

Griselinia littoralis

Arundinaria murieliae

Echium sp.

Yucca gloriosa

A plantsman's garden

OWNER: *John Codrington Esq. of Pimlico*

This backyard is a plantsman's garden and is the antithesis of a carefully manicured, symmetrically planned plot. Its enormous charm lies in its apparently neglected look. To the knowledgeable gardener, however, it is full of interesting and unusual plants, which are all allowed 'to do their own thing'. They are only checked if absolutely necessary.

Owner's gardening philosophy

'I think "mystery" is a very important quality to be sought after, and terribly difficult to achieve in the usual rectangular back garden. I am lucky, for my garden is *not* rectangular, but roughly the shape of a capital J. So it unfolds bit by bit as one comes along the stem of the J. Being of this unconventional shape it lends itself to wild gardening and naturalizing of plants which I think is, on the whole, my favourite form of gardening. I am naturally an untidy person and I should never be happy in a garden that had to be kept rigidly tidy and formal with no weeds (I call them "wild flowers") allowed. I think contrast of plant shapes is quite as important – almost more so than contrast or blending of colours.'

Dotted around and about are some medium-sized trees including *Ligustrum lucidum*, a handsome privet valuable for its size, shape and white-scented, autumnal flowers. This is indeed a welcome alternative to the more commonly planted evergreens of similar shape, although it does require protection from cold winds. Under the canopy of larger, more common trees, such as sycamore *(Acer pseudoplatanus)*, are shrubs *Elaeagnus pungens* 'Maculata', *Fatsia japonica*, *Genista hispanica*, Mexican orange blossom *(Choisya ternata)*, golden privet *(Ligustrum ovalifolium* 'Aureum'*)*, bay *(Laurus nobilis)* and *Mahonia bealei*, all left to their own devices.

There is hardly a patch of soil to be seen for ground-cover plants. There are carpets of several ivies including the marble-leaved variety *(Hedera helix* 'Discolor'*)*, *Euphorbia robbiae* – a charming species of the genus with yellow flowers in mid-summer and the very invasive *Lamiastrum galeobdolon*.

Two camellias feature in this backyard – *C. japonica* 'Apollo' with rose-red, semi-double flowers and the 'fish-tailed' camellia *(C. × williamsii* 'C.F. Coates'*)* which, as its common name suggests, has three-pointed ends to its leaves. This latter variety is of particular interest during the winter. Two bamboos have pride of place. *Arundinaria fastuosa* is the tallest growing hardy species but remains very compact and is the gardener's true friend, as its sturdy canes can be cut and used elsewhere in the garden. The other bamboo is *Arundinaria nitida*, a graceful and beautiful species whose canes arch, so weighted down are they by a mass of feathery leaves, some of which slowly turn yellow-green as the season progresses.

On the edge of the lighter part of the garden stands a Judas Tree *(Cercis siliquastrum)*. This deciduous tree has always been a favourite of mine, with its almost perfectly rounded leaves and rose-purple flowers, borne on naked stems in late spring. Near to it, out in the open, stands a mature *Hibiscus syriacus* 'Coelestis' whose leaves, as with all hibiscus, turn a delicious butter-yellow in the autumn.

Under the shadow of the trees lurks a wild olive, grown from a stone picked up in the south of France and pocketed by Mr Codrington. Although it will never fruit – commercial olive trees are grafted – this plant certainly makes an interesting conversation piece! Another less usual plant is found growing in amongst the gravel of

A wild garden which is allowed to do as it pleases, except when any one plant becomes too invasive. The plants have, however, been chosen with care by the owner who is a plantsman.

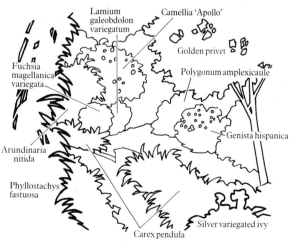

Lamium galeobdolon variegatum

Camellia 'Apollo'

Golden privet

Polygonum amplexicaule

Fuchsia magellanica variegata

Genista hispanica

Arundinaria nitida

Phyllostachys fastuosa

Carex pendula

Silver variegated ivy

the sitting-out area – the winter heliotrope (*Petasites fragrans*), which supplies welcome scented flowers in mid-winter. This woodland plant spreads voraciously and is perhaps better planted somewhere where it can have plenty of space. (This is not meant as criticism to the owner of this magical garden, but merely points out the general feel of his garden!) The winter heliotrope is joined by a native sedge *(Carex pendula)* which never fails to produce fascinating brown flowers during the summer. They are 3–4 ft (90–120 cm) in height.

Another rare, almost extinct, English plant is *Bupleurum falcatum*. It was known to have once grown in a hedgerow, between Ongar and Chelmsford, but may have been destroyed by road-widening. The seed was collected by the owner some years ago when it was quite plentiful. *Allium triquetrum*, a charming white flower, that has spread widely in Cornwall and the Channel Islands is sowing itself in the gravel, while everywhere is to be found the pretty yellow biennial called *Smyrnium perfoliatum* which comes originally from the Mediterranean, and is rarely seen in English gardens. It is at its best in late spring, although its parchment-coloured dead stems with their jet-black seeds are very attractive in late summer.

This tranquil spot must appeal to Mother Nature herself! Could the unexpected and uninvited appearance of *Scrophularia vernalis* on a rubbish tip have anything to do with this? After all, this endangered species of spring figwort is probably only to be found in one churchyard in Hampshire, and is a protected species. I would far rather believe that it arrived there by means magical, than on the gumboots of the garden's owner.

A garden designer's garden

OWNER: *Myles Challis Esq. of Leytonstone*

This backyard measures only 20 × 40 ft (6 × 12 m). It contains over 65 specialist plants, all chosen for their foliage. The owner, Myles Challis, is a garden designer who has always been interested in plants with bold and interesting leaves rather than flowers. As he pointed out, once the flowers have faded on the majority of plants, there's precious little left to look at. He has created this fascinating area as an 'organized jungle', although no plant is allowed to swamp its neighbour. He believes that no garden should be without water – there are two ponds here, one at the north end and one at the south, both linked by a stream which runs under the path. The path and the water features form a figure '8'. The pond nearest to the house is fed by a gentle trickle of water over a few rocks and the overflow is positioned at the other end of the garden by the water-loving *Gunnera manicata*.

When you are in this garden you are immediately transported to fairyland. You feel just like Alice must have done when she ate the piece of mushroom which Caterpillar had given her to reduce her size. Huge and wonderful leaves are all about and above you, and hardly one flower in sight!

It is always a bad sign when you see a visitor to a garden walking straight down the path without occasionally stopping. In this lush and exotic paradise you creep along at a snail's pace as there is so much to arrest the eye.

First to greet you is a fascinating and unusual poplar *(Populus lasiocarpa)*. It has the largest leaves of the genus (12×9 in (30×23 cm)) which are bright green with red veins. Beyond it is the beautiful *Rhododendron sinogrande* whose shining dark green leaves can grow as large as $2\frac{1}{2} \times 1$ ft

(0.8 m $\times 30$ cm), and are covered in silver-grey fur on their undersides. Its creamy-white flowers with a red blotch appear in huge trusses in mid-spring. Next is *Magnolia delavayi*, one of the largest leaved of all plants grown outside in mild areas of the UK. It produces all-too-ephemeral creamy white flowers measuring $6 \times 7\frac{1}{2}$ in (18×20 cm) in late summer and early autumn, and the variegated *Fatsia japonica* 'Variegata'. These plants set the tone of the garden. In this first section of the garden are many other esoteric plants to be seen. They include *Actinidia kolomikta* (a climber with leaves flushed with pink and white on the end), *Actinidia chinensis* (the Chinese gooseberry) with heart-shaped leaves and edible brown fruits, *Arundinaria viridistriata* (a Bamboo with dark leaves striped with rich yellow, on purple canes), *Cryptomeria japonica* 'Elegans' (a bushy conifer with feathery foliage which turns bronze during the winter), *Aralia elata* 'Variegata' (with huge pinnate leaves and white flowers in large pinnacles in autumn), *Viburnum rhytidophyllum* (a species with dark, glossy, corrugated leaves and small creamy-white flowers in late spring), *Cercidiphyllum japonicum* (whose round leaves turn yellow and pink in the autumn and when crushed, smell of strawberry jam). In this group can also be seen *Fagus sylvatica* 'Roseomarginata' (a variety of beech with pink-edged purple leaves), *Fatsia japonica* (with large, polished palmate, evergreen leaves and white, round flowers in autumn), *Corylus maxima* 'Purpurea' (the purple-leaved filbert), and *Acer macrophyllum* (the Oregon maple whose very large shiny leaves turn orange in the autumn).

The first pond to greet you, with the trickling cascade of water, has in its centre a submerged group of arum lilies *(Zantedeschia aethiopica)*. At its edge are planted the Indian bean tree *(Catalpa bignonioides)* with huge clear-green leaves, and up it is trained *Aristolochia macrophylla* with heart-shaped leaves, and fascinating tubular flowers in early summer. A New Zealand

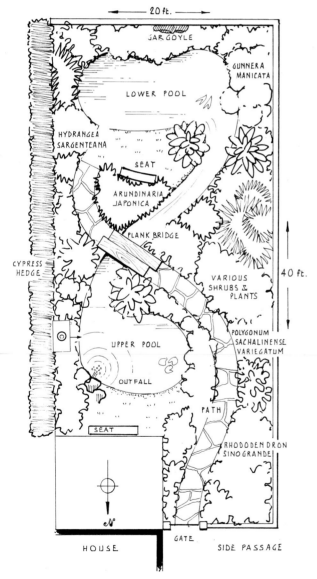

flax *(Phormium tenax)* with evergreen sword-like leaves and bronzy-red flowers borne on tall stems in summer sits in the corner and is flanked by *Viburnum davidii* (a small, compact, evergreen species with large leathery leaves and white flowers in early summer) on one side, and *Paulownia tomentosa* (which produces enormous leaves if coppiced every year) on the other. Along this east side of the garden is planted a hedge of Lawson cypress *(Chamaecyparis lawsoniana)*; slightly out of place but none the less an effective screen.

There are two ferns next to the water chute, *Athyrium felix-femina* and the hart's tongue fern *(Asplenium scolopendrium)*, as well as the common butterbur *(Petasites hybridus)*, so called as it was supposedly once used for wrapping up butter. Jutting into the pond on a shallow bank is a group of *Hosta seiboldiana* 'Elegans' (one of the largest-leaved and most magnificent of all the hostas). They grow under the canopy of a great white cherry *(Prunus* 'Tai Haku') which produces huge white flowers amongst coppery-red young leaves in the spring. Close by are two herbaceous perennials with magnificent large foliage, namely *Peltiphyllum peltatum* and *Ligularia veitchiana. Sasa palmata* (a rampant, large-leaved bamboo has been squeezed in as well!). On the other side of the path is a hardy banana *(Musa basjoo)*, *Rodgersia tabularis* (with huge circular leaves) and a magnificent knotweed *(Polygonum sachalinense* 'Variegatum', a herbaceous perennial capable of growing several yards (metres) tall in a season, with delightful yellow-variegated leaves).

Where the stream goes under the path there is a barrier of taller growing plants: *Arundinaria japonica* (bamboo sp.), the golden elder *(Sambucus racemosa* 'Plumosa Aurea') and the windmill or Chusan palm *(Trachycarpus fortunei)*. In front of them are two tree ferns *(Dicksonia antarctica)*, and three more herbaceous perennials with dramatic foliage, *Trachystemon orientale, Ligularia hessei* and *Rodgersia podophylla.* This barrier has been planted in such a way as to make one or two carefully positioned dramatic plants visible through it. These include *Gunnera manicata* (with immense rhubarb-like leaves), assorted skunk cabbages *(Lysichitum* spp.), *Catalpa × erubescens* 'Purpurea' (with dark purple young leaves and shoots), and yet another *Ligularia*, this time *wilsoniana*.

As you walk through the bamboo you are greeted by a *Hydrangea sargentiana*, a species with very large velvety leaves, and much of the rest of the plant is smothered in bristles and hairs. It has large, bluish, 'lace-cap' flowers in mid-late summer.

At this point you find a welcome seat where you can compose yourself and attempt to recover from the after effects of vegetative euphoria! Staring at you from the other side of the second pond is a gargoyle which is flanked by the unvariegated *Polygonum sachalinense*, a royal fern *(Osmunda regalis)* as well as the rare purple cultivar *(O. r.* 'Purpurascens')*, and – something commonplace for a change – a common silver weeping Birch *(Betula pendula)*. Also evident are *Parrotia persica* (with flaking older stems and crimson autumn colour), a mouthful of a maple *(Acer velutianum vanvolxemii* with enormous five-lobed leaves), *Ligularia dentata* 'Desdemona' and a beautiful fern *(Polystichum setiferum* 'Divisilobum')*. Over the water the ivy-clad trunk of a dead laburnum leans a little ominously, and a ginger *(Hedychium gardnerianum)* tickles your right ankle.

This garden could be described as many things. It is fantastic, in the true sense of the word. However, it would be difficult for the layman to emulate it owing to the difficulty of obtaining many of the plants which can only be bought from specialist nurseries.

A garden which is devoted to plants with dramatic foliage. Any flowers which appear are considered an extra bonus, but by no means important.

Trachycarpus fortunei

Prunus 'Tai Haku'

Arundinaria japonica

Polygonum sachalinense 'Variegatum'

Peltiphyllum peltatum

Hosta sieboldiana 'Elegans'

An artist's garden

OWNER: *R. B. Kitaj Esq. of Chelsea*

This is not the sort of garden you would expect to find in the heart of a large city! How refreshing to find a woodland landscape especially designed to fit into a space measuring 82 × 20 ft (25 × 6 m).

Owner's gardening philosophy

'My first principle of gardening is never to touch anything in my garden. My gardener does all that and when she tells me what something is, I tend to forget what she told me. I wanted my backyard to look like a piece of woodland without flowers; just greenery, but my gardener sneaks some flowers in anyway'.

A sunken path meanders through the garden and disappears into the distance. The garden thus loses clearly defined depth and the visitor is lured onwards. The end of the path leads directly into the yawning mouth of a Second World War air-raid shelter, beckoning one on even further into the bowels of the earth.

Wherever you look, ground cover is thick and consists of several different species of ivy, Periwinkle (*Vinca* sp.), *Pachysandra terminalis* 'Variegata', bracken, woodruff (*Asperula odorata*), *Geranium macrorrhizum*, *Helleborus foetidus*, *Muehlenbeckia complexa*, *Heuchera* 'Greenfinch', *Polypodium vulgare* and many others. They all grow between miscellaneous stones and rocks which have been collected from trips to the seaside and other places, including the pavement outside! The upkeep is kept at a minimum by these ground-cover plants which smother even the most determined weeds.

The shrubs and trees dotted about include a bamboo (*Arundinaria murieliae*), *Garrya elliptica*, *Robinia pseudoacacia* and the common sycamore (*Acer pseudoplatanus*), the latter is occasionally checked to stop it taking over. One of the few flowering plants to have been 'sneaked' into this delightful setting is the stinking iris (*I. foetidissima*) whose vivid orange/red seeds are a delight during the autumn and first half of winter. (It is, after all, a woodland plant.) Another is *Allium triquetrum* whose white, bell-shaped flowers stand 1 ft (30 cm) high over the green woodland carpet in early summer.

(*Opposite*) This wild garden includes a meandering path which leads into the mouth of a Second World War air-raid shelter. The planting consists of thick ground cover, with a heavy accent on leaf, not flower. You would never think you were in the heart of Chelsea.

An escapist's garden: area 1

LOCATION: *Notting Hill*

Although this is just one part of a larger garden, it is a very good example of an ideal layout for an invalid confined to a wheel chair. It is raised and therefore adds extra interest. It is an open area and its whole 'point' hinges on the grouping of a few special trees. They are all medium-sized and thus suitable for a small garden. Access is made easy up the winding ramp, with one or two plants tumbling over the higher wall which make the journey more interesting. In the far corner, we see the ever-popular *Robinia pseudoacacia* 'Frisia' whose bright yellow/green leaves persist throughout the summer, never failing to look fresh until the first frosts. In front is a more unusual tree, a weeping elm *(Ulmus camperdownii)* which contrasts well with the stag's horn sumach *(Rhus typhina)* behind. In the other corner stands a taller-growing silver birch *(Betula pendula)* with its characteristic white bark. This low-maintenance area illustrates how decorative a group of trees can be on their own.

As the owner of the garden puts it 'The path was created in response to my wish for a surprise within the garden'.

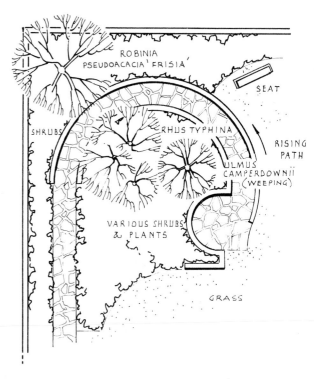

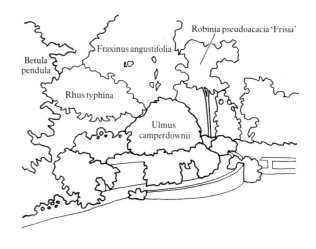

24

This is in fact part of a larger garden. The ramp illustrates a
sympathetic treatment for invalids in wheelchairs. The group of
trees at the top have been carefully chosen so that their foliage
complements each other.

A designer's garden

OWNER: *Professor Bernard Nevill of Chelsea*

The whole feeling of this garden is one of tranquil informality. The house to which this garden belongs was once lived in by G. P. Boyce and many of the plants and trees which he planted in 1869 (as recorded in his diary) survive today. These include the fig, wisteria and vine, the latter scrambling over the pergola. There is also a 300-year-old mulberry, one of the very few left of the original plantings during the seventeenth century in a vain attempt to start up a self-sufficient silk industry in Britain.

The owner of this historical backyard is a great believer in evergreens to supply something of interest during the winter. Accordingly, there are some fine camellias and an evergreen magnolia, amongst others.

Other features in this garden are the fountain, which sits in a blue bowl inlaid with gold mosaic and the trellis, which is a famous one, designed by Norman Shaw.

Owner's gardening philosophy

'I am a great believer in the Jekyll/Robinson concept that gardens should blend into houses and am totally in sympathy with their idea of the *wild* garden. i am endeavouring to create the impression of a wild herbaceous border in front of the red brick wall by planting delphiniums, hollyhocks, sunflowers, phlox, larkspur, foxgloves, lupins and pinks. I believe that a red-walled garden should have red terracotta ornaments and I have been collecting terracotta urns for some time: I hope to find a life-size terracotta statue to place at the end of the pergola . . . I hate gladioli, formal bedding and in fact most new forms of old-fashioned varieties.'

A totally relaxing and informal garden. There is nothing here to alarm, but everything to soothe.

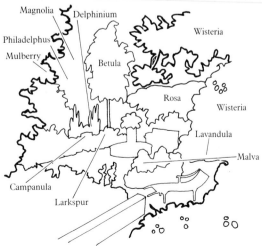

Magnolia
Delphinium
Philadelphus
Mulberry
Betula
Wisteria
Rosa
Wisteria
Lavandula
Malva
Campanula
Larkspur

A clever solution of what to do with the corner of a garden (belonging to Miss Jane Egerton-Warburton, p. 30). The angle of the mirror succeeds in reflecting a feature which is not otherwise immediately visible.

2

THE
LANDSCAPED BACKYARD

All gardens should be 'landscaped' inasmuch as a drawing on paper helps you to decide where to position the various features you want to include. For this style of garden, which usually contains many different features, the drawing ought to be to scale as it is then much easier to gauge the quantity of materials needed.

First, survey the site with a good long tape. The direction of north should be clearly shown as this will indicate areas which get little direct sunlight and will inevitably determine your choice of plants (see list of shade-tolerant and other plants, p. 89). Ideally, a soil sample should also be taken. The canopy spread of existing trees should also be clearly indicated for the same reason. If the ground slopes the change of levels will have to be gauged in order to find out how many steps will be needed and whether it will be necessary to build a supporting wall, etc. Existing drains and underground cables should always be shown on the plan, as their presence could well change the shape you had originally envisaged.

Once you have finally decided on a plan which meets all these requirements, you can then transfer it from the paper into the garden showing shapes of borders, size of lawn, etc., with white string tied to pegs. Remember to include lighting and other electric installations in your plan as the laying of the underground cables is one of the first things to do. Indicate their whereabouts with canes to avoid interfering with them while the rest of the garden is being built. Electric cables can of course be pinned neatly to the boundary wall or fence, at a later date. The next task to be undertaken is the building of walls, patios, ponds and other 'hard landscape' features. This is usually the most depressing part of the whole exercise. The building-site appearance of the garden is not helped by aching backs and fraying tempers, nor by finding out you've run short of something on half-day closing!

Once the cement bags and other mess have been cleared away, and the soil has been improved by digging in plenty of organic matter, planting can begin. Try to plan your programme so that this stage coincides with very early spring or autumn. An empty garden is capable of swallowing up an enormous quantity of plants and even once they've been positioned in their allocated spot there always seems to be far too much bare earth about! If this is the case you have probably planted correctly as, however tempting it may seem, planting too close together causes headaches in later years.

Except in more tropical climates there is no such thing as an 'instant' garden, unless you go to the expense of buying semi-mature stock. I always give a new garden at least five years to start looking presentable. During these first years bedding plants and fast-growing annuals (see plant list, p. 91) can fill any gaps. Finally, it is well worth mentioning to the investor that a properly landscaped garden always adds a great deal of value to any property.

A hidden garden

OWNER: *Miss Jane Egerton-Warburton of Chelsea*

(Garden designed by Mike Bell)

This backyard makes an excellent summer sitting room.

The existing raised platform at the end has been extended to provide a larger seating area. Leading up to it are curved steps built with Old London Stock bricks.

To give the garden more depth a mirror has been incorporated with an arched frame surround which appears to lead through a trellis screen. The mirror has been off-set diagonally across one corner. It not only reflects the water plants in front, but also various other plants, depending on where you stand.

This garden was completed only a month before the photograph was taken. Eventually climbers, including various clematis and jasmine species will cover the trellis around the arched mirror. The basic structural planting of *Cordyline*, *Camellia* and rhododendron species are supplemented in the summer by pink busy Lizzy (*Impatiens*), fibrous begonias and zonal pelargoniums ('geraniums'), petunias, nicotianas and other annuals.

Owner's gardening philosophy

'A small garden requires a great deal more attention than a large one where some untidiness can be lost in size. Continual dead heading and feeding are essential. Colour is most important in a small space. I try to keep my colour scheme to a maximum of three, preferably two, pink being a good choice as there are so many different shades and varieties of plants. This with small patches of blue or grey foliage can look most attractive.'

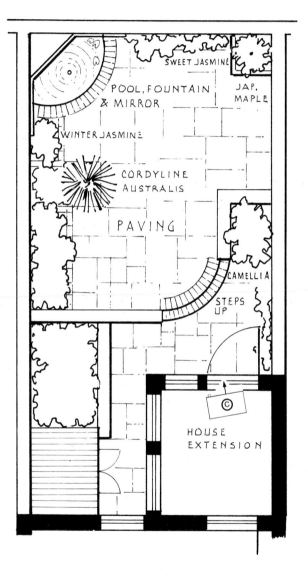

30

The same garden as shown on p. 28. A lovely view to wake up to
from the bedroom window, to beckon one down to breakfast.

A family garden: 1

LOCATION: *Notting Hill*

This backyard was once a garage. The entire area was smothered with concrete and extraneous buildings, a view commanded by the kitchen window. Something had to be done to make the washing-up ritual a more enjoyable one!

The client has several children and so it was important that these seemingly indefatigable little dears were catered for as well as creating a prettier view. Her philosophy on small space gardening is: 'The layout must be as simple and unfussy as possible, with a few choice specimen plants ringing the seasonal changes'. A plan was drawn to scale to cater for these requirements and a rectangular pergola walk with a 'bicycle circuit' around the edge materialized. The one metre wide beds were excavated with the help of a pneumatic drill and refilled with fresh top soil with plenty of organic matter in the bottom. The existing surface drain coincided with one of the edges of the rectangular bed, which solved the problem of drainage. The upright posts were 3×3 in (8×8 cm) throughout and the horizontal timbers were 2×2 in (5×5 cm), with fashioned ends.

This sunny area proved to be a most successful playground for climbing plants! Nearer to the house where there is less direct sunlight were planted common jasmine *(Jasminum officinale)*, Virginia creeper *(Parthenocissus quinquefolia)*, *Rosa* 'Mermaid', 'Gloire de Dijon', 'Danse de Feu' and 'Emily Grey' (all shade-tolerant roses) and *Garrya elliptica*.

In the sunnier part were planted *Fremontodendron californicum*, *Abutilon megapotamicum*, *Wisteria sinensis* 'Alba', *Clematis* 'Nelly Moser', *Clematis × jackmanii*, *Hydrangea petiolaris*, *Lonicera × americana*, *Chimonanthus praecox*, *Cytisus battandieri* and passion

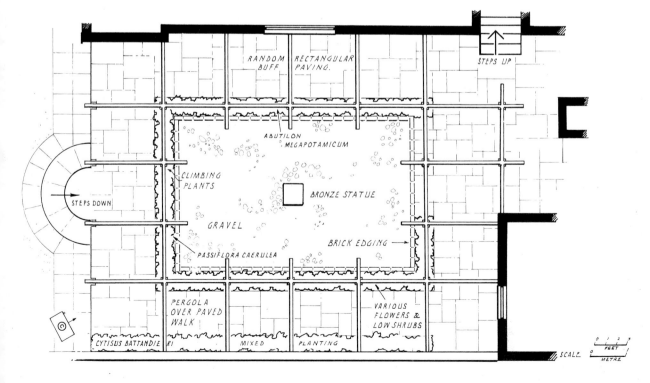

flower *(Passiflora caerulea)*. The plants and shrubs between the posts include *Camellia × williamsii* 'Donation', purple New Zealand flax *(Phormium tenax* 'Purpureum'), common rosemary *(Rosmarinus officinalis)*, *Cotoneaster horizontalis*, Mexican Orange Blossom *(Choisya ternata)*, foam flower *(Tiarella cordifolia)*, various hostas, *Bergenia cordifolia* and miniature roses.

The central area is covered with 3 in (8 cm) of pea-shingle. It is contained by a single row of bricks set on edge and was chosen for its cheerful pink colour. It needs very little maintenance, i.e. it is raked once every few weeks and acts as an excellent 'carpet' for the focal point at the centre – a sculpture by Nicola Godden called 'Kira' which succeeds in adding the final touch.

(Above) The remains of a three-car garage . . . *(below)* transformed into a rectangular pergola walk. The back wall has been removed to give access to the rest of the garden.

A designer's garden

LOCATION: *Pimlico*

(Garden designed by Pamela Bullmore)

If you look at the before and after photographs of this backyard you will find it difficult to believe they are one and the same. The main reason for this metamorphosis are the two brick circles which kiss in the middle. They demonstrate a very clever way of making a mere 16 × 59 ft (5 × 18 m) look very much larger than it really is. The brick herring bone pattern (with 1100 bricks per circle) has been laid with 10 mm joins throughout – I would have hated the job of cutting those bricks at the edge of each circle! The bricks were laid after the ideal preparation for the use of all paving material. That is, the depth of soil removed was first carefully gauged to allow for hardcore at the bottom covered in 3 in (8 cm) of concrete. The bricks themselves were then laid on ½ in (1.3 cm) mortar. If someone were ever to press the wrong button, I imagine this area would remain intact throughout the holocaust. Gentle slopes were carefully gauged to ensure efficient drainage away from the house. The circle further away from the house presented drainage problems however, and a soakaway was built in at the very base of the end seat – at the base of this wall you can see the small gaps which allow the water in. This soakaway consists of 3 in (8 cm) of gravel over hardcore and, under that, a generous addition of lime was mixed with the clay to help break it up.

There's nothing run-of-the-mill about the plants in this garden either. As the owner put it 'the pleasure lies in seeing each plant as an individual, and in getting close enough to it to observe its nature, smell its scent, however delicate or faint, and to watch it changing. I find it is easy work to keep the garden fresh – plenty of house-keeping, looking for pests – especially slugs and snails

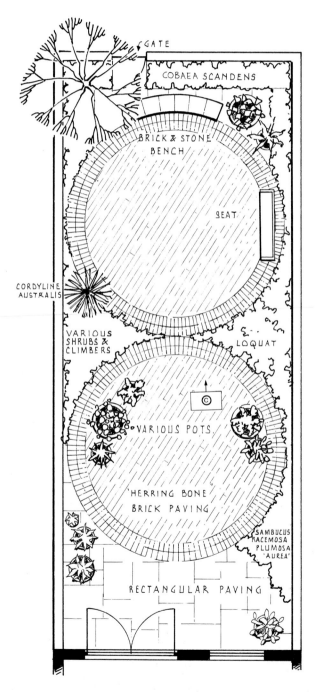

GATE

COBAEA SCANDENS

BRICK & STONE BENCH

SEAT

CORDYLINE AUSTRALIS

VARIOUS SHRUBS & CLIMBERS

LOQUAT

VARIOUS POTS

'HERRING BONE BRICK PAVING

SAMBUCUS RACEMOSA PLUMOSA 'AUREA'

RECTANGULAR PAVING

(*Right*) A familiar sight indeed to anyone moving into a new house . . . (*below*) metamorphosed into a beautiful backyard. The two circles of herring bone brick paving contain 1100 bricks each and just kiss in the middle. They succeed in making the garden look very much larger than it really is.

of which we have plagues—snipping off dead bits, and watering or just sprinkling the leaves with water to wash off dust, all make this garden a little oasis of contentment. There's nothing like watering on a hot summer evening to make London seem quite bearable.'

At the very end is planted a cup and saucer vine *(Cobaea scandens)*, a half-hardy climber planted only too seldom, especially as it is ideal for milder parts of the country. *Cobaea* flowers turn from a greenish white to purple and its thick growth does an excellent job of masking the ugliest of walls, and can be grown as an annual for the greenhouse in colder parts of the country. Also to be found at the end of the garden is a *Hydrangea villosa*, a really stunning late-flowering variety, the climbing rose 'Madame Alfred Carrière', a group of pink and purple *Helleborus orientalis* and, in the middle, the Himalayan cow parsley *(Selinum tenuifolium)* which has lacy foliage and huge cow parsley flowers in summer.

The small beds, formed like a triangle with two curved sides, contain groups of plants which complement each other. In the most shaded one we see *Helleborus × sternii*, *Hosta fortunei* 'Albopicta', the hart's tongue fern *(Asplenium scolopendrium)*, Solomon's seal *(Polygonatum × hybridum)* woodruff *(Asperula odorata)*, an ideal ground-cover plant for damp areas under trees, with fragrant white flowers in late spring/early summer and yet another spectacular fern, *Dryopteris pseudomas*. Standing over these esoterica is a golden elder *(Sambucus racemosa* 'Plumosa Aurea') whose deeply cut, golden foliage makes a welcome addition to any garden.

A group of plants in the middle on the left includes *Euphorbia characias wulfenii*, *Trachelospermum jasminoides*, *Acanthus spinosus*, *Rheum palmatum*, *Cordyline australis* and pale-coloured apricot foxgloves, all under the protection of a climbing *Akebia quinata*. On the corresponding side, the beautiful arching branches of that special bamboo, *Arundinaria nitida*, catch the eye. It is unexpectedly joined by a loquat *(Eriobotrya japonica)* and Dutchman's pipe *(Aristolochia macrophylla)*.

A plant which deservedly crops up more than once in this garden, full of unusual and interesting plants, is the hardy variegated fuchsia *(F. magellanica* 'Versicolor'), with its beautiful white and green leaves blotched with pink, and red and purple flowers. This deserves a place in a pot on any patio. A few carefully chosen containers act as host for some special inmates. Here, we have a very special fern, the soft shield fern *(Polystichum setiferum* 'Densum'), and next to it a most unusual thornless holly *(Ilex aquifolium* 'J. C. van Tol' syn. *I. a.* 'Polycarpa') which has been clipped into tiers and takes pride of place near the entrance of the garden, justly chosen as the first eye-catcher. Other plants in pots are *Hosta* 'Thomas Hogg' and *Philadelphus* 'Sybille'. Near to them on the wall can be seen growing white *Solanum*, *Vitis coignetiae* and pink-flowering *Clematis montana*.

Much can be learned from this garden.

An artist's garden

OWNER: *David Holmes Esq. of Ealing*

This is a good demonstration of how to disguise the side wall of an ugly garage or brick wall. Rather than merely covering it with climbing plants this sort of 'hard' landscape treatment is far more effective and much easier to maintain.

The arch in the centre is made of brick slips. This not only supplies a false door to the facade, but also frames the mask of the fountain which would otherwise look a little lost all on its own. A submersible pump drives the water from the pond to the mask. The height of the mask was carefully gauged as these pumps can only take a certain weight of water, according to their size. The correct length of pipe must also be calculated. If it is too long, the pump will not be able to cope with the amount of water it is forced to circulate.

The pond is surrounded by interesting plants. On the left is a dwarf bamboo (*Arundinaria viridistriata*), *Fatsia japonica*, *Ligularia* 'Othello', *Anemone hybrida* 'Alba', the purple form of New Zealand flax (*Phormium tenax* 'Purpureum'), and under the apple a group of geranium 'Johnson's Blue'. On the right, we see the same dwarf bamboo with a group of *Artemisia* 'Lambrook Silver' immediately to its right. Grouped around the Japanese maple (*Acer palmatum*) can be seen a combination of *Salvia nemorosa* 'Superba' and lavender (*Lavandula* 'Hidcote').

On the far right is an *Amelanchier lamarckii*, whose new spring leaves are a yellowish dark-green, splashed with pink (and which also has rich autumn colouring). This is underplanted with four *Potentilla fruticosa* 'Abbotswood'.

In the pond itself there is a small water lily (*Nymphaea alba* 'Minor'), and on the other side *Typha minima*.

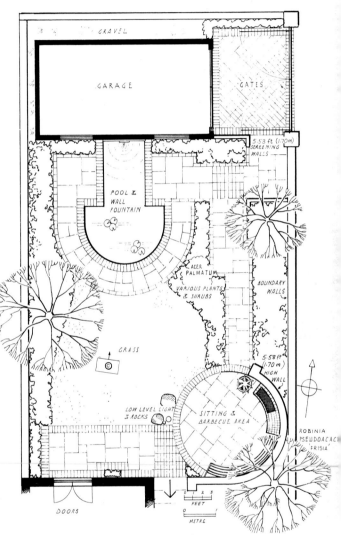

Owner's gardening philosophy

'The need to create some seclusion from the roadway that runs on three sides of the house led us to the plan we carried out. We wanted a sort of secret garden, something unexpected. Somewhere to potter, eat, laze and entertain – a true extension of the house. I'm happy mowing a lawn so we have some grass, but the garden is mainly stocked with perennials and evergreens.

I wanted real York stone pathways so that, with the existing old stone walls and ivies, we'd be half way to a mature-looking enclosure. The children are grown-up so a pond was very important. Apart from its tranquilizing effect, water in a garden is a constant source of interest, ecologically too. No garden should be without one. Two very happy frogs magically appeared from nowhere.'

Interesting treatment for a shed or garage. There are endless variations on this theme to meta-morphose an otherwise drab wall or building.

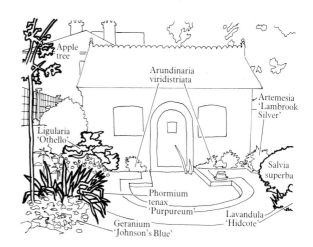

A garden for all seasons

OWNER: *Mrs Angela FitzGibbon of Clapham*

This backyard measures 30 × 20 ft (9 × 6 m). It is a good example of evergreen planting. As you can see the plants have been packed in! Many of these shrubs will have to be removed – thinned out, as it were – once they start to impede each other's progress. No doubt, the designer had this in mind when he designed this garden for his client.

This planting plan reflects the owner's philosophy on gardening in small spaces: 'I regard a small town garden visible from the house as an extension of the ground floor, i.e. as an extra room. It must therefore look good throughout the year. Evergreens of various shades and textures are ideal, while colour can always be added in summer with bedding plants. An outside tap is essential.'

The evergreens include *Pieris formosa forrestii* and *P. japonica* 'Variegata', *Cotoneaster horizontalis*, *Euonymus* spp., *Olearia* spp., *Senecio greyi*, *Elaeagnus pungens* 'Maculata', *Rhododendron* spp., *Cistus* spp., and the Chusan palm *Trachycarpus fortunei*. Deciduous shrubs include *Pittosporum* spp., *Cornus* spp., *Weigela* spp. and *Hydrangea* spp.

At the back are two gleditsias and a silver weeping birch. The fountain in the middle consists of a rendered and water-filled void 18 in (45 cm) deep with a submersible pump at the bottom, covered in pebbles. Small children love to run through the jet of water and they can be left to play on their own safely as the pebbles prevent there being any depth of water. Once the children have grown up the pebbles could be removed and be replaced by one or two water-loving plants.

This fountain is ideal for children who love to jump through the jet. There is no water depth as the concrete sump is filled with pebbles. Once the children have grown up the pebbles can be removed.

A working mother's garden

OWNER: *Mrs Philippa Bradley of Hampstead*

(Designed by Pamela Bullmore)

What first struck me about this backyard was its clever use of plants and materials. The area is 93 ft (28 m) long and 30 ft (9 m) wide where it meets the house. It gradually tapers to a mere 10 ft (3 m) at the end through the arch. As you leave the French windows, the first area you come across is paved with grey paving stones and basket-weave squares of old brick. This paving treatment is always very effective.

The visitor is lured further up some steps, built of the same brick and paving mixture, blending the two areas. On either side of the path which follows on is an area generously mulched with an attractive pinkish pea shingle. Through the gravel can be seen growing *Euphorbia characias wulfenii*, various pinks (*Dianthus* spp.), *Hebes*, two formal clipped bays *(Laurus nobilis)*, a small pink-flowering hydrangea, *Agapanthus* sp., *Senecio* 'Sunshine' pink-flowering rock roses *(Helianthemum* sp.), *Schizostylis coccinea*, *Lavandula* 'Hidcote', *Piptanthus laburnifolius* and a small, striking pampas grass.

The third area you come across (and so far you are totally unaware that the garden is becoming slowly narrower), consists mostly of lawn and the borders contain some interesting low-maintenance, foliage plants such as *Pieris formosa forrestii*, the smoke tree *(Cotinus coggygria)*, *Weigela, Daphne odora, Escallonia macrantha, Mahonia* 'Charity', Mexican orange blossom *(Choisya ternata)*, *Alchemilla mollis* and *Elaeagnus pungens* 'Maculata'.

At the end of the lawn is an informal arch through a screen of ivy and honeysuckle beyond which can be seen an expanse of gravel and the hint of a rockery. This very informal barrier performs a most important

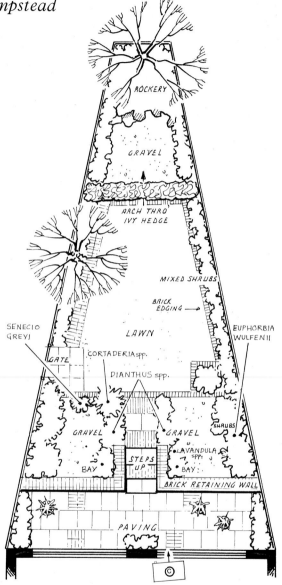

role – it cuts off the end of the garden from view and, by doing so, manages to disguise the shape of the plot, which would otherwise look somewhat like a slice of cheese.

The rockery houses such plants as *Aucuba japonica, Tellima grandiflora* 'Purpurea', azaleas, *Bergenia* 'Ballawley' and *Acanthus mollis*. Here there is an ivy *(Hedera canari-*

A cleverly planted wedge-shaped garden which tapers from a width of 30 ft (9 m) to 10 ft (3 m). The tapering edge to the lawn, which runs parallel to the perimeter fence, helps to create a false perspective. The arch near to the end lures the visitor on further.

ensis 'Variegata' syn. *H.* 'Gloire de Marengo'). This plant is a very good example of how many plants with variegated leaves (especially holly species), will produce beautiful pure off-white leaves, if deprived of direct light. All in all, when the visitor to this garden eventually returns to the house, he feels as if he has been on quite a long walk, an illusion brought about by the clever and different treatment of each area.

The author's previous garden

LOCATION: *Chiswick*

Backyards of this shape are commonly found belonging to 'working-class' houses built at the turn of the century. It consists of a narrow side passage alongside the kitchen, with a small area measuring 15 × 16½ ft (4.5 × 5 m) at the end.

Only one year ago it was a neglected dump which boasted a spectacular range of miscellaneous rubbish. As this back part of the house faces north, the narrow side passage in particular, gets very little sunlight for most of the year. A Chinese Virginia creeper (*Parthenocissus henryana*) was planted in the shadiest spot of all. This beautiful climber comes into its own when planted in deep shade as the white veins on its leaves really stand out under such conditions. Further along the fence, was planted *Garrya elliptica* 'James Roof' alongside a climbing *Hydrangea petiolaris*. Always try to get hold of this variety of *Garrya* as it is a showy plant with extra long catkins in winter.

Here, the wall of the house was as messy as the garden had been. It consisted of black down pipes, orange window sills and dark-red lintels. Everything was painted the same colour, i.e. off-white, to give it uniformity and the area more light.

I am not a believer in small lawns so the end of the garden was laid down with pea shingle with three borders, one raised, around the edge. At the same time, a round dais was built to accommodate the small nine-sided greenhouse, destined as the focal point. A rounded trellis arch was built where the passage meets the end garden. When the garden is viewed from the dining room window the apex of the greenhouse meets exactly with the centre of the arch.

The most shaded border accommodates *Euphorbia characias wulfenii*, hostas – *Hosta* 'Thomas Hogg' and *H. sieboldiana*, *Crocos-*

mia masonorum, *Pieris formosa forrestii* 'Wakehurst', cotton lavender (*Santolina*), foxgloves and another climbing hydrangea (*H. petiolaris*) – all safe bets for a north-facing aspect. The bench is covered with a simple arbor made of 3 × 3 in (8 × 8 cm) posts with a 'roof' consisting of slats of wood to support climbing plants. A hardy outdoor eating black grape (*Vitis vinifera* 'Brandt') has been trained up one side, and *Clematis × jackmanii* on the other. On the small, sunny triangular bed on the right hand side of the

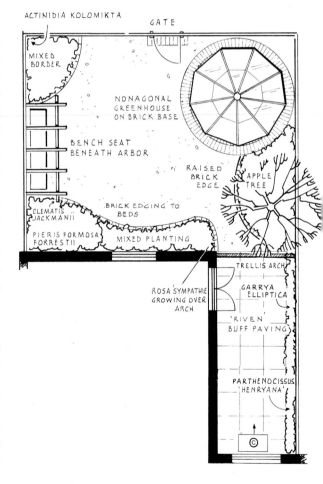

My dog, called Flowerpot, and I. The greenhouse was positioned so that the apex stands in the centre of the arch. It also acts as the focal point, albeit a little large in proportion to the rest of the garden.

bench is a common rosemary *(Rosmarinus officinalis)*, a lavender *(Lavandula* 'Hidcote'), *Actinidia kolomikta, Carex pendula* and assorted annuals.

Also planted in this small bed is a hybrid blackberry, planted because of its vicious thorns and delicious fruit. (There is a service lane beyond the fence and I did not like the idea of uninvited intruders thinking this is an easy way in.)

The west-facing border underneath the apple tree has been planted up for colour. Here we see *Tradescantia × andersoniana* 'Flore Pleno', *Thalictrum dipterocarpum, Convolvulus tricolor, Liatris callilepis, Rudbeckia fulgida, Crocosmia masonorum, Gazania × hybrida* 'Bridget' and lupins. There is a newly planted climbing rose 'Golden Showers', which is to be trained up the apple. A white wisteria *(W. sinensis* 'Alba') is planted on one side of the trellis arch and *Rosa* 'Sympathie' on the other. Opposite the back door were placed pots containing herbs.

Wall to wall foliage

OWNER: *Mark Hudson Esq. of Fulham*

This backyard measures 18 × 16 ft (5.5 × 5 m). The U-shaped raised border at the back not only supplies instant height but also a marvellously lush backdrop for the rest of the garden.

It was filled with fresh top soil and planted up with shrubs and trees including Mexican orange blossom *(Choisya ternata)*, *Fatsia japonica*, assorted camellias, a peach, an ornamental crab apple, and *Eucalyptus niphophila*. A 'Kiftsgate' rose (perhaps the most rampant of all climbing roses) has been allowed to invade wherever it chooses, re-inforcing the tropical jungle atmosphere of this delightful backyard.

Six gothic pillars stand guard around the sides. They are made of trellis (to Kenneth Turner's design) and support *Clematis montana, Clematis × jouiniana*, a grape vine and Dutchman's pipe *(Aristolochia macrophylla)*.

Thirty-two large terracotta pots are dotted all over the place, which mainly contain colourful annuals.

This area was designed to look like a 'well-furnished room' for the summer. It certainly feels like it.

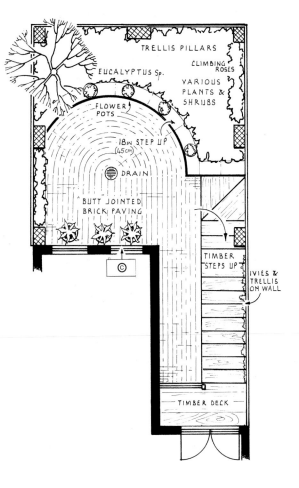

44

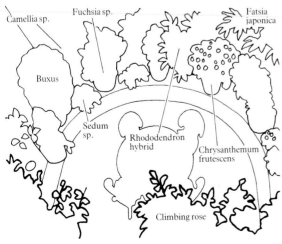

Camellia sp.

Fuchsia sp.

Fatsia
japonica

Buxus

Sedum
sp.

Rhododendron
hybrid

Chrysanthemum
frutescens

Climbing rose

An aerial view of a backyard with a horseshoe-shaped raised border. The top of the supporting wall acts host to pots containing colourful annuals and houseplants during the summer.

A summer sitting room

OWNER: *Mrs Norma Heyman of Chelsea*

Basically, this garden contains three paved areas each on a different level. The largest in the centre provides plenty of room for entertaining whilst the smallest, nestled in the far left corner, was designed as a hide-away sitting area – somewhere to escape to from the rest of the world. This hide-away can only be reached via one of the two paved paths which have plants growing across them purposely, in order to herald the rustling arrival of intruders. The whole end of the garden, the paths and the hide-away, had to be planned carefully as a common lime tree casts shade over most of the area and drips glue in typical fashion on everything underneath. Evergreen plants with strong and thick leaves were chosen for this area. They include *Griselinia littoralis*, camellias, rhododendrons, *Phormium* spp. mahonias and bamboo, all of which do become rather black and discoloured during the latter half of the summer, but recover and seem happy enough, despite everything.

Just escaping the canopy of the lime is *Magnolia wilsonii* whose delicate white flowers hang like bells (and not like candelabra, like the majority of this beautiful genus). A cabbage palm *(Cordyline australis)* is well suited to the urn, out of which it seems to be exploding like a firework. The two pairs of steps are flanked on the left by a black mulberry *(Morus nigra)* and, on the right, by a *Robinia pseudoacacia* 'Frisia'. This sort of garden I would describe as 'semi-wild' – a very good design for such a shape, i.e. long and thin. Mind you, I designed it.

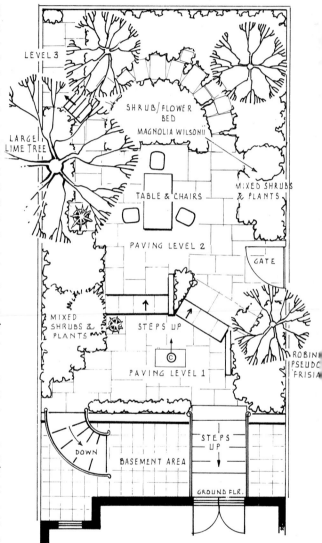

This is the central section of a three-level garden.
Two paths lead on further either side of the
mahonias to beckon the curious visitor on
further.

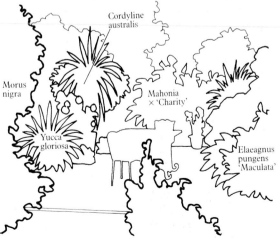

Cordyline
australis

Morus
nigra

Mahonia
× 'Charity'

Yucca
gloriosa

Elaeagnus
pungens
'Maculata'

3

TROMPE L'OEIL
BACKYARDS

Trompe l'oeil is one of those French expressions which translate clumsily into English. 'Something that deceives the eye' is the best dictionary definition I can find. This art can be executed with a variation of materials: paint, mirror, trellis shapes laid flat onto walls, etc. Plants play an important role with all of them. Here are some hints for the would-be amateur muralist.

Murals

An amateur artist can paint a mural in his own garden, either to hide an ugly wall or just to add interest and beauty to his garden. The first task is to prepare the wall:

Filling

Brick walls have grooves or ridges where the mortar is, so it is best for the whole area to be cement-rendered, i.e. covered with a smooth layer of cement. This is a difficult operation and should be done by someone with experience. If the area is not large, it could simply be filled and smoothed over with a suitable outdoor filler using a trowel.

Cement-rendered or concrete walls obviously don't need rendering because they are smooth already, but they may need filling (as above) if the surface is old or degenerate. Remember that it is very difficult to paint a good picture on a rough surface.

(Opposite) This *trompe l'oeil* mural has romantically embellished what a mirror could achieve. It shows a slightly angled view of the back of the house and the arch (in the background), also 'mirrored', reflects the fastigiate conifers (Robert Lacey's garden, p. 50).

Every effort should be made to ensure that the wall is as dry as possible inside, both from the point of view of rising damp and of rain etc. Paint is more likely to peel because of internal moisture than the weather!

Coating

Allow the cement or filler to dry thoroughly, then coat with a masonry stabilizer, which is a transparent liquid, possibly toxic when wet, followed by white masonry paint. Alternatively, a neutral sealer (a kind of thick white paint) can be used in place of the above two treatments – this will prevent any alkali from the wall affecting the paint. The surface is now prepared.

(*Note*: There are many different products on the market, and they may differ from one country to another, so if you're not sure, or the instructions are not clear, consult a professional builder about the effects of a given product.)

Paints and glazes

The best paints for this type of work are high-quality artists' acrylics. You just need a bucket of water for mixing and cleaning, and these paints dry almost immediately to a permanent, waterproof finish. A couple of coats of artists' acrylic varnish will then seal the painting completely.

Mirrors

Mirrors can perform wonders and last a long time out of doors, so long as they are properly treated. Sadly, mirrors for outside use are involved far too little in landscaping. They can come in particularly useful in a small backyard where they can reflect extra light, especially when artificial lighting is turned on during the evening. Mirroring to be used for outdoors must first of all be heavy duty. Their silvered backs must be thoroughly protected from the elements with several applications of red oxide bitumastic paint. The edges should be taped (bitumastic tape) to prevent water from gaining access through the sides. Brick is a good surface onto which mirrors can be attached. As brick is absorbent, it helps to soak up any dampness.

A mirror can always be positioned in such a way as to reflect a plant (or statue) which is not actually visible from the house because it is deliberately obscured by something else. If that mirror was the same size as a door, the end result would look as if it was indeed (an open) door with the plant or statue beyond. A flat structure suggesting false perspective can be achieved.

Plants can assist in creating false perspective in many ways. A small statue at the end of the garden can be flanked by, for example, two dwarf conifers which would be 'to scale'. Ivies and other trained plants can become a strip of lawn leading to an arch beyond (p. 54). I have also seen this done with pyracantha. The mural on p. 53 is made all the more realistic by the presence of plants forming a loose curtain of irregular growth in front. There are many other methods of achieving successful optical illusions so I leave the rest to your imagination.

A biographer's garden

OWNER: *Robert Lacey Esq. of Chelsea*

This tiny backyard measures only $11\frac{3}{4} \times 15$ ft $(3.5 \times 4.5$ m$)$, and yet it appears to be very much larger, because of the clever layout. The delightful *trompe l'oeil* arch contains a mural pretending to be a slightly angled mirror. It reflects the back of the house, one side wall up which *Wisteria sinensis* has been trained and the daffodils in the foreground. The arch in the background is also 'mirrored' and it reflects the conifers.

The ledge to the left of the *trompe l'oeil* arch comfortably houses a string of terracotta pots. Apart from a few spring bulbs all the other plants are evergreens: *Fatsia japonica, Hedera canariensis, Camellia* spp., *Phormium tenax* 'Variegatum', the lesser periwinkle *(Vinca minor)*, various ferns *et al.*

There are many pots dotted about. They contain rhododendron species, an evergreen magnolia *(M. grandiflora)*, the daisy bush *(Olearia × haastii)*, *Camellia × williamsii* 'Mary Christian' in the potty, and assorted ivies. The palm in the pot to the right of the arch is the Chusan palm *(Trachycarpus fortunei)* and this is joined by a lollypop bay. The lovely, warm terracotta colour of the wall was brought about by mixing a terracotta red paint with a little yellow ochre and plenty of white. The white diamond-shaped trellis pinned to it is set off most effectively.

This garden was only planted up less than a year ago and it was photographed in early spring – the dream of an instant garden come true!

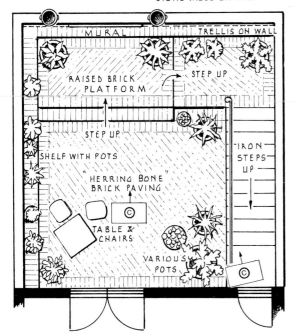

STONE VASES ON WALL TOP

MURAL

TRELLIS ON WALL

RAISED BRICK PLATFORM

STEP UP

STEP UP

SHELF WITH POTS

IRON STEPS UP

"HERRING BONE" BRICK PAVING

TABLE & CHAIRS

VARIOUS POTS

The view from a basement dining room window. The delightful mural will help both digestion and conversation.

An artist's garden

OWNER: *Roy Alderson Esq. of Chelsea*

This is a flat wall, apart from the horizontal balustrades and the statue, which are only one foot proud from the wall. Will you ever be content in having a plain wall at the bottom of your backyard again? This is *trompe l'oeil* at its best, made even more realistic with the use of (clever) planting. The top pinkish section has been painted on melamine, which consists of compressed layers of paper. Considering pink is a fugitive colour, it has lasted remarkably well after 15 years. The lower half, which incorporates the steps is painted with acrylic with a little yellow ochre, on plaster. This has been touched up since it was first painted, but only very little.

The planting in this yard is simple yet effective. By far the most important roles are played by the climbers. They are common jasmine *(Jasminum officinale)*, the common blackberry, Chinese Virginia creeper *(Parthenocissus henryana)*, common ivy *(Hedera helix)*, the golden hop *(Humulus lupulus* 'Aureus'), and vine species. They are allowed to grow as they wish although the jasmine is encouraged (in particular), so that

it will eventually surround the entire garden. It is also encouraged to grow in front of the steps to give the impression that it is tumbling down them.

Of course, the eye is immediately arrested by this end wall, but the sides are interesting as well. On one side, the wall is flanked by busts of Apollo, young Augustus and Julius Caesar and on the other a somewhat unlikely couple – Diana and an unknown Victorian Lady! They sit on plinths and at their feet informal woodland plants such as ferns and campanulas are joined by the occasional rose.

This backyard can be further transformed for parties when it becomes an exotic, jungle-like, tented room. A hand-painted plastic awning can be unfurled from a boon which is attached to the top of the wall at one end and the house at the other. Brightly coloured birds and plants are depicted against a brilliant blue sky and even the balustrading has been painted along the bottom, so that it continues along the sides.

This is the work of a man with exceptional talent, Roy Alderson, whose philosophy on his backyard is 'To form an amalgam of garden and drawing room so that it is difficult to tell where one begins and the other ends'.

(Opposite) It is almost impossible to believe that this is a flat wall apart from the balustrades and the statue which are only one foot proud of it. This is *trompe l'oeil* at its best.
(Left) The same backyard is transformed into a room for special evenings, The painted canvas tented ceiling is unfurled from the boom which is suspended over the garden.

An eastern potentate's garden in Chelsea

This tiny yard measures only $5\frac{3}{4} \times 10$ ft (1.75×3 m). It has very high walls on either side and before this was built, an ugly view of several back windows.

The client wanted something that was 'green and pretty and nice to look at. Lit up at night to give a festive air'. The problem was solved by constructing a *trompe-l'oeil* panel of trellis. The green 'path' in the foreground consists of an ivy chosen as an ideal plant for this totally shaded area. The ivy was planted in such a way as to deceive the eye, i.e. to look like a path leading up towards the oriental arch in the centre. It is regularly clipped during the summer to preserve the neat edges to the 'path'. They are planted in individual pots so that they can be replaced in case of a fatality. They are arranged on a stepped wooden framework, the top step being the same width as the central 'far-away' arch.

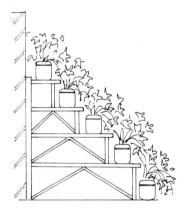

Both the trellis and the back board are painted white. To add more interest, two climbers, *Akebia quinata*, with their delicate five-lobed leaves, have been planted on either side in their own individual pots, in order to break up the trellis. This climber will survive in complete shade, but will have larger leaves and produce dark purple, sausage-shaped fruits if planted in a sunny position.

(*Left*) This sunless, tiny backyard is designed in such a way as to make the ivy look like a green lawn leading up to an arch in the distance, tapering as it goes. The back panel is thus 'pushed' right back.

An escapist's garden: area 2

LOCATION: *Notting Hill*

What better treatment for the end wall of a row of terraced houses than this acrylic mural by Tim Plant! There's nothing to beat the classical. The Taj Mahal with the strip of water in front and the avenue of perfectly matched fastigiate trees. I very much like the preening pelicans in the foreground and the tiger, whose tail wanders off the panel to join the plants. The border directly underneath the mural contains many lush and verdant plants which must be negotiated to get to the great building. The willow on the right and sycamore on the left slightly obscure the edges of the vista and by so doing they make it all the more realistic.

This mural has succeeded in 'pushing' this garden right back well beyond the wall at the end. The trees either side frame the vista.

A grandmother's garden

OWNER: *Mrs B. J. Dowling of Wimbledon*

This charming backyard measures only 13¾ ft (4.25 m) across and 21¾ ft (6.5 m) deep. It faces north-west and therefore gets little direct sunlight. This means of course that the pond is suitably placed, as direct sunlight causes water to become a murky green. The use of materials and plants is varied which makes it a 'busy' area, and it seems larger than it really is – the eye is kept busy as it darts from one thing to another. The rose climbing up the left-hand wall of the garage is 'Madame Gregoire Staechelin' which never fails to supply a generous supply of blooms in late spring, and is covered in quantities of large orange hips well into the winter as well. The only disadvantage of this rose is that the branches are brittle, and need tying back before they get too long.

The entrance to this delightful spot is flanked by *Cryptomeria japonica* 'Elegans' on the left, and *Cornus alba* 'Spaethii' on the right, Behind the *Cryptomeria* is one of the most beautiful ornamental grasses, *Miscanthus sinensis* 'Gracillimus', which is tucked in behind a boulder. Further in towards the mirror a bamboo *(Arundinaria nitida)* plays an important part in this mini-landscape. A rhododendron is tucked away in the far left-hand corner. In amongst the pebbles set between the paving stones, are the stinking iris *(I. foetidissima)*, a wood-land plant with evil-smelling flowers and delightful bright orange/red seeds in the autumn, two hostas, *H. sieboldiana* and *H.* 'Thomas Hogg', the low mound-forming ornamental grass *Minuartia*, an ornamental member of the rhubarb family *Rheum palmatum* 'Rubrum', one of the most grace-ful of all the beautiful ferns, *Polystichum setiferum* 'Densum' and *Acanthus spinosus*. The main feature of this tiny area are the framed mirrors consisting of three panels,

attached to the back wall. The frame is a cast-iron Victorian porch laid flat, and painted white. The mirroring has been properly protected for outside use and as the owner says 'we wanted mirrors to give that added illusion of space, softened by the original Victorian wrought iron'.

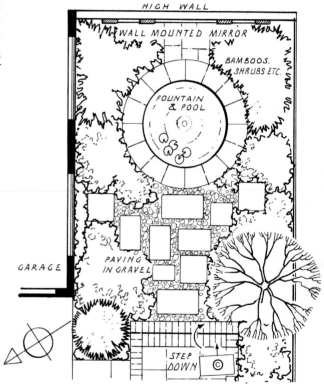

The back wall of this charming backyard has affixed to it a wrought iron Victorian porch laid flat. The gaps of the arch have been filled in with heavy duty mirror, thus creating an extra vista.

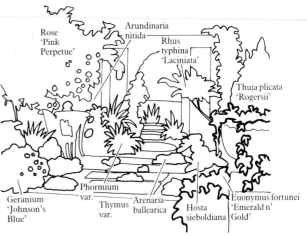

Rose 'Pink Perpetue'

Arundinaria nitida

Rhus typhina 'Laciniata'

Thuja plicata 'Rogersii'

Geranium 'Johnson's Blue'

Phormium var.

Thymus var.

Arenaria ballearica

Hosta sieboldiana

Euonymus fortunei 'Emerald n' Gold'

A family garden: 2

LOCATION: *Notting Hill*

When the owners of this property moved in they were presented with the problem of how to make the view out of their dining room more attractive. All they had was a very tall and dark brick wall within 8 ft (2.4 m) of the window. This wall was the direct result of an extension built onto the back of the neighbouring house – a common enough problem these days in large cities. Although the resulting wall faces west, it is completely shadowed by the rest of the house. I was invited in to remedy this problem as the client was worried about the possible digestive difficulties of her dinner guests.

Shade-tolerant climbing plants such as the climbing hydrangea *(H. petiolaris)*, Chinese Virginia creeper *(Parthenocissus henryana)*, etc., were considered but it was agreed that the end result would not add any much-needed light to the area.

I eventually decided to create a *trompe l'oeil* using trellis and mirrors, using a plan drawn to scale. If this is not done at the very beginning, it is impossible to work out how it is going to fit, what size of mirror should be cut and exactly what quantities of materials are needed.

The construction of the rounded sections of the trellis frame were made by first bending to shape four $\frac{3}{16}$ in (5 mm) strips of deal. This is done by soaking or steaming them and bending them onto a frame around strategically positioned nails. Once dried they are glued and pinned together. A design with straight lines only can be made of 1 in (2.5 cm) square strips of softwood (if it is to be painted) or hardwood (if it is to be stained).

The end result is supposed to give the impression that three walkways lead on through the wall to give extra depth.

The paving here is Bradstone Cotswold Riven which replaced the much gloomier York crazy paving. A recessed inspection cover was introduced containing the same pavers. This alternative to a man-hole cover is altogether neater and can easily be lifted if necessary with two keys.

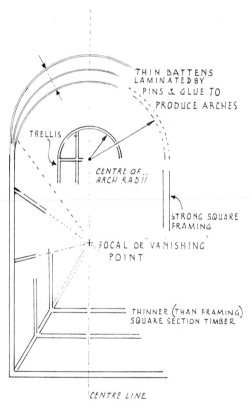

THIN BATTENS LAMINATED BY PINS & GLUE TO PRODUCE ARCHES

TRELLIS

CENTRE OF ARCH RADII

STRONG SQUARE FRAMING

FOCAL OR VANISHING POINT

THINNER (THAN FRAMING) SQUARE SECTION TIMBER

CENTRE LINE

Diagram showing construction of *trompe l'oeil* trellis frame.

These mirrored *trompe l'oeil* panels have 'rescued' the view out
of a dining room window which would otherwise consist of a
gloomy, bare wall.

This delightful domed, wrought-iron gazebo acts as an excellent
and effective focal point in this charming garden
(John Junner, p. 62).

4

FOCAL POINT BACKYARDS

A garden, of whatever size, can seem empty and unanchored without something on which the eye can immediately focus. It is all the more important to establish a focal point in a small urban garden as this prevents the eye from wandering over the fence into the neighbour's plot! Although the choice of focal point is personal, such a feature should always be visible from a window which is used a great deal.

Antique statuary etc. can be prohibitively expensive, a very special plant can act as an eye-catcher, preferably one which can be admired all the year round. An evergreen plant in a very beautiful pot is another idea. Only too seldom used as a focal point is a bench surrounded by an arbor (see p. 84). Over this can be trained a winter- and a summer-flowering climber. It is not only functional, but comparatively cheap to build, and the acquisition of a bench should be thought of as a life-time investment. Long, thin gardens are commonplace and cry out for a point of extra interest to remove any possible feeling of a corridor. If the sides are literally smothered with plants and a special feature is positioned at the end, the shape can be disguised. The effect can be ruined if the fountain, statue or other feature is too large. The smaller it is, the further away it appears to be – it is merely a question of getting the scale right. The impression of extra depth can be further enhanced by planting larger-leaved plants in the foreground and plants with small leaves at the end.

Don't allow the main feature at the end of the garden to steal the show and also position a few interesting plants and objects along the route. In the case of very long and thin gardens it can look most effective if the route to the end is dead straight and built of different materials. It can start off as paving, then stepping stones through a pond, through an area of gravel and on to the end stretch via an arch. Creating separate areas, each with it own individual treatment, is a very effective way of making a small garden seem larger than it is.

'. . . a stately pleasure dome decree . . .'

OWNER: *John Junner Esq. of Kensington*

This is a small backyard which measures only 18 × 30 ft (5.5 × 9 m). The layout has been cleverly thought out by its owner, obviously a man with a discerning eye. An area of this size desperately needs something very special as a focal point. Here, we see a majestic gazebo made of wrought iron, painted white. It not only dominates the garden, but also holds it together. Similarly, a backing screen of trees or trellis covered in evergreen is a great asset, a mixture of contrasting evergreen plants providing winter interest.

This philosophy is reflected in the garden itself and it is obvious that much thought has been given not only to the plants themselves, but also to their positions. When the present owner took it over this garden had been an overgrown mess and neglected. To the left of the gazebo is a mature *Fatsia japonica* which was found amongst the jungle and carefully restored, staked and pruned. It now adds a special contribution to a relatively new planting. The backyard would now be looking too bare if everything had been removed to begin with (a useful tip to remember if you have just inherited an overgrown patch). A fast-growing weeping cherry was removed from the centre of the garden and replanted against the back wall directly behind the gazebo. It now forms an elegant back-drop. Another lesson can be learnt from this – central planting of large-growing trees in small spaces always proves a mistake because the mature tree will shade and take over the entire area.

On the far right stands a golden Irish yew (*Taxus baccata* 'Fastigiata Aureomarginata'), a useful evergreen tree for shaded areas. It is flanked by a variegated rhododendron (*Rhododendron* 'President Roosevelt') – a variety only too seldom planted, and it's a

safe bet that the conversation over a cup of tea under the gazebo will include 'How interesting! I've never seen a variegated rhododendron before'. Another rhododendron to be found in this garden is the delightful *R. yakushimanum* species which has pleasing felt on the undersides of its leaves. There are a number of climbing roses in this backyard including 'New Dawn' which covers the gazebo. Other varieties include 'Mermaid', 'Copenhagen' and 'Peace'.

The lawn in the centre of the garden is not

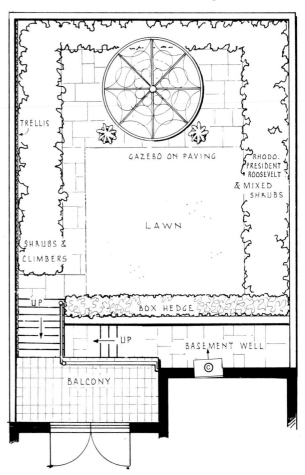

The decorative and ornate gazebo in white-painted wrought-iron
is lightly sprinkled with the delicate flowers of *Rosa* 'New Dawn'.

a feature I would agree with. It is far too small and must be very difficult to keep immaculate. However, the owner is forgiven as he had to have some grass to remind him of his old garden in the country!

Against the sunny side of the house is planted one of the most delightful of all sun-demanding climbers, i.e. *Fremontodendron californicum*. It is semi-evergreen, retaining most of its delightful palmate leaves in a mild winter and its waxy, five-petalled yellow flowers are produced throughout the entire summer, from late spring to mid-autumn.

The owner of this garden has managed to overcome the problem of identifying plants for curious visitors. He staples their labels onto a large piece of cardboard to coincide with the plants' positions in the garden. A clever idea, indeed, for all owners of gardens of this size – a faded and illegible label is always annoying.

A country woman's London garden

OWNER: *The Countess of Westmorland*

This is a backyard with a difference. It measures only 20×30 ft (6×9 m). Ground level is three feet higher than the sitting room floor and it coincides with the bottom of the windows through which the garden is viewed. The focal point is an arbor over a bench with a plaque on the back wall. The arbor is framed between two clipped box (*Buxus sempervirens*), planted in Italian terracotta pots.

Owner's gardening philosophy
'The basic design and structure is symmetrically planned and disciplined. Informal, jungle-like plants can then be positioned around the garden haphazardly, with pots and tubs full of colour and scent in the centre'.

The area at the end surrounding the arbor is paved with brick in a basket-weave pattern and this contrasts well with the pea shingle in the foreground. Two different sorts of paving in a small area always suceed in making it seem larger than it really is.

The garden is dotted with larger camellias, *Eucalyptus* and graceful bamboo (*Arundinaria murieliae*). The two charming trellis 'dividers' on either side help give extra dimension.

The entrance passage to the garden at the side of the house has been most successfully covered in white trellis, making an otherwise insipid corridor into an inviting one (p. 85).

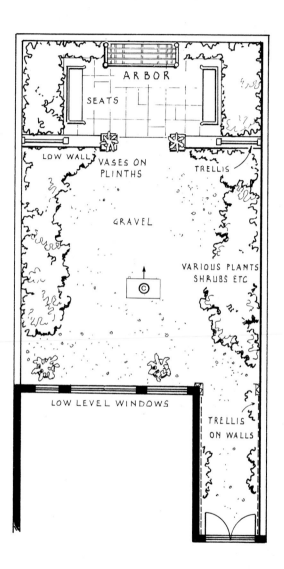

(Opposite) The arbor-like trellis over the bench 'anchors' this pretty backyard.

A green room

LOCATION: *Pimlico*

This backyard is an awkward shape and measures only $14\frac{1}{4} \times 16\frac{1}{2}$ ft (4.5×5 m). It faces due south. The back wall has a slant which has been successfully squared up using a series of staggered trellis panels. This has solved the problem of what to do with the pointed far left-hand corner.

This delightful small area orientates entirely around the focal point – a tiered fountain consisting of stone scallop shells, fed at the top by a spouting cherub. (The submersible pump is in the sunken square pond beneath).

The owner wanted the garden to act as an extension to his house. Thus, the choice of herring-bone brick paving with its suggestion of a Persian carpet. The garden is planted in such a way as to look green throughout as much of the year as possible and the presence of water induces a relaxed, serene atmosphere. At the end, on both sides of the fountain, are ivies, *Hedera helix*

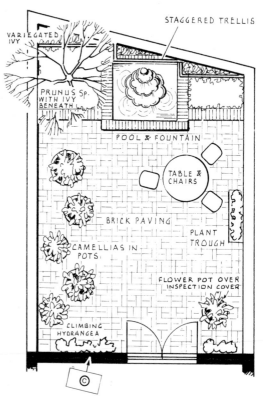

The charming tiered fountain not only catches the eye, but also soothes as it trickles.

'Buttercup', 'Goldheart' and 'Sagittifolia'. They are used both as ground cover and as climbers to clothe the otherwise insipid trellis. In the left-hand corner is a winter cherry (*Prunus subhirtella* 'Autumnalis') which flowers throughout much of the winter. Against the left-hand wall is a selection of container-grown camellias, all chosen for their pale pink flowers. These include *C.* × *williamsii* 'Donation', 'Bow Bells' and the variegated 'Golden Spangles' and *C. japonica* 'Lady Clare' and 'Tricolor'. Once they have finished flowering in mid-spring, they are pushed back against the wall and potted zonal pelargoniums ('geraniums') are put in front of them. The camellias thus continue to be useful throughout the summer (and winter) as a colourful backdrop for bright annuals. This is the only part of the garden which is allowed colour.

A banker's wife's garden

OWNER: *The Viscountess Hardinge*

This backyard measures $21\frac{1}{2} \times 43\frac{1}{4}$ ft (6.5 × 13 m) and the planting is only a couple of years old. Its whole point is the magnificent fountain, which is made of lead and originates from Rome. The small round pond at its base is 8in (20cm) deep and concrete-lined. It is surrounded by brick work laid frog-down in a radiating pattern and has been pointed in all but a few places, where the resulting gaps have been planted up with 'cushion' plants. These include the creeping peppermint, penny royal *(Mentha pulegium)* and *Ajuga reptans* 'Burgundy Glow'. Other plants of similar creeping habit were intro-duced – *Saxifraga* 'Cloth of Gold' and the chocolate-coloured clover, *Trifolium repens* 'Purpurea'. In the corners under the retain-ing walls can be seen *Hosta fortunei* 'Albo-picta' and ferns *(Dryopteris pseudomas)*. On the shady side of the garden can be seen soft orange, amber and buff candelabra primulas *(P. bulleyana)*, whilst on the sunny side are pale blue and bronze bearded iris.

In this backyard the eye is first arrested by the lead, tiered fountain in the centre. The radiating brick around it then causes the eye to veer towards the varied and lush planting all around.

5

TERRACED BACKYARDS

Very often, it is simply impractical to level a sloping backyard, as the soil cannot be left to bank up against the house, causing damp problems. The prospect of carrying soil by the bucketful (through the house) is enough to make one think again. Why not take advantage of the lie of the land and transform it into a terraced garden?

A plan to scale on paper is again vital for the planning-out of a sloping garden, the main reason being the inevitable construction of steps. Each riser should be of a comfortable height (about 6 in; 15 cm), and treads must be sufficiently deep (about 1 ft; 30 cm).

Many terraced gardens will require supporting walls. They must be sufficiently strong. Sadly an ordinary half brick wall with foundation will not suffice!

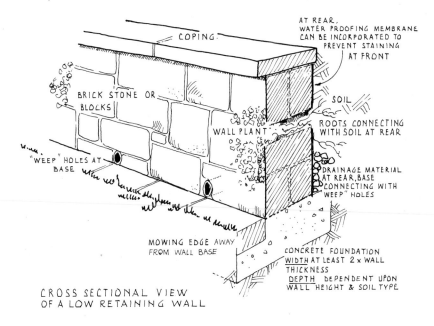

CROSS SECTIONAL VIEW
OF A LOW RETAINING WALL

(Opposite) This highly individual terraced backyard (belonging to Zandra Rhodes, p. 70) is full of surprises including mirrored mosaics, garlands of scallop shells, Tibetan pillars and attractive pots.

69

A fashion designer's garden

OWNER: *Zandra Rhodes of Paddington*

This backyard is extra-something, 'extraordinary' is not strong enough to describe it. A unique imagination and special eye are responsible for the detail.

Only plants with white flowers were chosen. These include *Hosta elata* and *H. plantaginea*, *Helleborus niger* and snowdrops. Plants without significant flowers were also chosen for their contributions of lush and verdant growth, i.e. baby's tears *(Helxine)*, the soft shieldfern (*Polystichum setiferum* 'Densum'), and the sensitive fern *(Onoclea sensibilis)*.

The focal point is a reclining figure – a Mexican Chac Mool – which is to be found at the top of a ziggurat (or stepped dais). Much of the concrete is smothered in mirror mosaic which removes most of its grey hard-

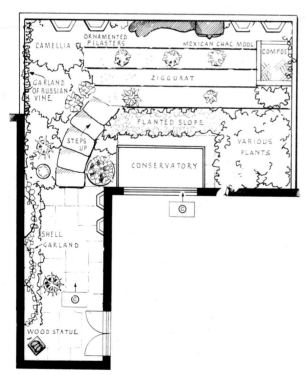

ness and gives it a light feeling in both senses of the word.

'These two features (the Chac Mool and the Ziggurat) combine to make a small London back garden become something grand because these big things in it somehow have a reverse effect on the smallness.' Directly in front of the Chac Mool stand four pots, each containing a white flowering shrub. These are a camellia, *Rhododendron yakushimanum*, a cornus and a hydrangea. (I was intrigued to see a compost heap for household waste, tucked in beside the Aztec figure.)

This garden gets no sun at all. 'Then the challenge of a garden with no direct sunlight got to me. First the Ziggurat is ideal for potted plants, second plants needing acid soil like camellias, azaleas etc. have to be potted up specially as they don't always like the native soil. Until that time I was not hooked on gardening and started to look at other people's gardens with similar woodland conditions.' The other many eye-catching features include Indian pillars made of fibre glass and painted in many colours. These are to be found against most of the walls in the garden. Garlands of scallop shells are swagged above columns of mirror mosaics with a climbing hydrangea (*H. petiolaris*) in between.

Further into the garden a small conservatory juts out. It contains some of the more tender ferns including the stag's horn fern (*Platycerium bifurcatum*) and *Nephrolepis exaltata*. On the floor 'swim' two black plastic swans smothered in walnuts and hazel nuts. They have taken on a new lease of life as cache-pots.

Between the conservatory and the next garden, Russian vine (*Polygonum baldschuanicum*) has been tied in a single swag supported on wire. This is cut back several times during the summer – on average once every three weeks. Naturally, there is nothing as mundane as trellis fence here. There are several plastic plants in the garden, mostly ferns. First thing every morning Zandra Rhodes goes out armed with a watering can and talks to her living plants. Most surprising of all is that the eye never once looks up at the tall buildings which surround this backyard, in fact one is not aware of them at all.

The focal point is more than aptly supplied by a Mexican Chac Mool at the top of a Ziggurat (or stepped dais). Note the compost bin on the right—a sign of a good gardener.

Owner's gardening philosophy

'This garden is designed to have very little upkeep, but it takes one day a week to keep in order, fed etc. I wanted to have a fabulous evergreen garden to look good with minimum upkeep. I love grandure, the excessive grandure of things like the hanging gardens of Babylon! Things like the fact of my garden being walled in by such high walls and facing a high wall I found a challenge. They led me to "involving" that wall and putting pots on it and ornate columns on the part of it facing my house. I never tire of the beauty of waking up and hearing a bird sing in the garden or listening to the rain coming down (which is why I want the trickle of a fountain). I believe too, that no "dead" backyard is unconquerable'.

A flowery boscage

OWNER: *Colin Wells-Brown Esq. of West Brompton*

The builder and owner of this terraced backyard is an accomplished gardener of several decades' experience, and it shows. Some considerable time was spent on planning this garden, first of all on graph paper, and then with white pegs and and string. This important preliminary precaution has resulted in perfect proportion and scale – a lesson to us all.

Thought was given first to the centre of the site. From previous experience, the owner found that if you plan from the outside boundaries inwards, the central area of the site tends to result in a void. This explains the position of the gently trickling fountain with the tiny pond below, and two planting areas for herbaceous plants and shrubs apart from the boundary beds. These beds can be circumnavigated so that they can be viewed from every angle. There are also some interesting varying levels.

Despite the fact that the paths are only 18 in (45 cm) wide, there is seldom 'congestion' as there is always an alternative route. The lower patio is fed by two pairs of steps and these meet at the top at a sitting-out area.

One plant which features heavily in this garden is busy lizzie (*Impatiens* spp.). They flower continuously from planting time in late spring to the first frosts, and can be bought as small plants in flower, so that the buyer can be sure of the flower colour. This gardener considers fibrous begonias as equally good value. The large white and yellow flowers of the tuberous begonias are always raised every year for this backyard as they never fail to add a splash of intense colour to the more shaded areas. They are started into growth in trays of damp peat in the basement of the house. Above them are suspended four fluorescent tubes within a

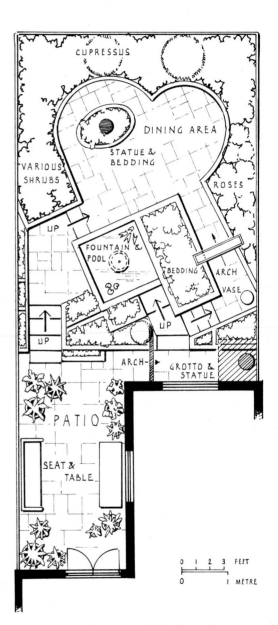

(Above far right) An aerial view of a terraced garden with carefully planned levels and walkways. *(Far right)* A clever layout to this terraced garden offers alternative routes for the visitor to take.

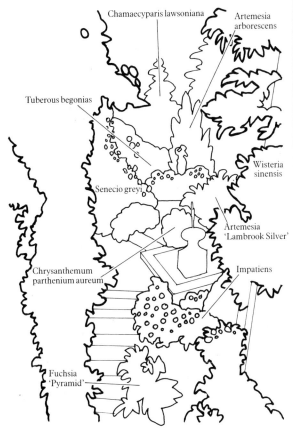

Chamaecyparis lawsoniana

Artemesia arborescens

Tuberous begonias

Wisteria sinensis

Senecio greyi

Artemesia 'Lambrook Silver'

Chrysanthemum parthenium aureum

Impatiens

Fuchsia 'Pyramid'

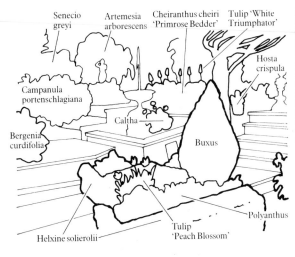

Senecio greyi

Artemesia arborescens

Cheiranthus cheiri 'Primrose Bedder'

Tulip 'White Triumphator'

Hosta crispula

Campanula portenschlagiana

Caltha

Bergenia curdifolia

Buxus

Helxine solierolii

Tulip 'Peach Blossom'

Polyanthus

home-made reflector. A time switch ensures that they receive the optimum 14 hours of daylight and the end result is firm, dark green, shrubby growth.

Another plant always used here every year is honesty *(Lunaria)*, whose white or purple flowers ensure a good splash of colour during the first part of the summer. Many of their seed heads, which look like silver 'moons', are left as they supply decoration for the first part of the winter. These 'moons' do, however, need peeling apart to reveal the bright silver membrane within. This is described by the owner as a 'sherry job': '. . . that is, it is one that, with a little practice, can be performed with one hand leaving the other free to hold a glass of sherry'. A useful occupation for a pre-prandial stroll.

Colour is controlled in this garden: 'The eye is best pleased by a general view that may contain perhaps as little as 10% bright colour, with a generous backing of shades of green and perhaps silver'. The master of this garden is a strong believer in all varieties of ivy as a backcloth for other climbers, and as a screen to supply privacy. He grows jasmine, roses and clematis over the ivy and also hangs pots on ivy-clad walls. These containers eventually become hidden and the fuchsias which grow in them 'burst forward in delightful pendant bouquets'.

Mostly pale colours are chosen for the more shaded areas as they show up the best in such conditions. The many conifers and evergreens in this garden play an important part as a backcloth to plants with silver foliage. The beautiful *Artemisia arborescens* is featured heavily as a result, and one is planted somewhere near to the centre of the garden where it attains an average height of 8 or 9 ft (2.5 m) after three or four years. It is a tender perennial which will not survive a severe winter in the micro-climate of London.

Each bed has its own colour mixture. Pale mauve, pink, white and pale yellow are all together in one, while the rose bed behind the herbaceous border is a mixture of all the reds, pinks and mauves, underplanted with nicotianas and petunias.

For scent, *Jasminum polyanthum* with its white and pale pink flowers from mid-spring to early summer, is hard to beat. The owner, who is also trying out the orange-scented *Pittosporum tobira*, has failed with the Chilean bell-flower *(Lapageria rosea)* and is about to introduce the beautiful blue plumbago as well as *Dipladenia splendens*. These are always grown as greenhouse plants in less mild climates.

Because the garden is visited daily, watered and fed during the summer, its occupants all have large smiles and grow and grow! As a result they need to be staked. This is undertaken a group at a time and the operation does not prove to be 'too much of a bore'. 'It is in this task that the imaginative gardener can perhaps show his greatest skill in maintaining and improving the elegance of plant growth and in instilling into the garden an overall sense of poise, of unruffled peace, an ephemeral quality of seemingly tireless beauty, a quality that must totally exclude any evidence of the violence of man or nature; where all is serene, graceful and relaxed.'

Owner's gardening philosophy

'Some people seem to think that they can call in a specialist to design for them a beautiful garden and that then they will have a beautiful garden for ever. This is not true at all. The garden designer can do a great deal, but the long-term result must depend absolutely upon the person who maintains the garden. It is an endless succession of decisions both great and small. What to cut off and what to leave on, what to leave loose and what to tie back'.

6

VERY SMALL BACKYARDS

The various methods of creating a false illusion of space are all the more important when designing a tiny backyard. Very small areas can, in many ways, be much more difficult to plan as only very special plants and objects must be chosen. The plants must be positioned in such a way as to rid the area of its box-like feeling. A false impression of extra depth can be achieved by staggering plants so that the eye rests on one and then on to the others behind.

There is a popular fashion for painting boundary walls white. In a very confined space this can be disastrous as the exact size of the area immediately becomes only too obvious. More successful is camouflage of boundary walls or fences in a mass of carefully chosen plants.

Make sure that there are several interesting little plants tucked in behind something else (a fern behind a pot, through which can be seen protruding the nose of a stone hedgehog, for instance), so that everything in the garden is not immediately visible upon first entering it.

Although it is a general rule that, if a small space is crammed with too many bits and pieces it looks messy, in some cases it seems to work. Potted plants are ideal where space is very limited as they can be moved around to more prominent positions when they are looking their best. One or two interesting evergreens can always be brought into view during the bleak winter months as well. *Trompe l'oeil* (p. 49) can be very useful where there is limited room as can mirrors for outdoor use (p. 50). These small gardens are often treated as an extension to the house – an outdoor summer room, if you like.

A doctor's garden

LOCATION: *Battersea*

This tiny L-shaped south-facing garden is a delight. Although it faces due south it only gets sun in the very early morning and from mid-day until dusk, because of a high wall on its southern side.

Upon first entering this backyard you are met by a variety of plants in tubs and troughs. These are *Buddleia* 'Lochinch', *Hedera colchica* 'Paddy's Pride' (growing up the trellis opposite the door), *Cytisus × kewensis*, *Convolvulus cneorum*, *Santolina neopolitanum*, purple sage (*Salvia officinalis* 'Purpurascens') and silver thyme, all crowded together and overflowing their container underneath the kitchen window. A plumbago

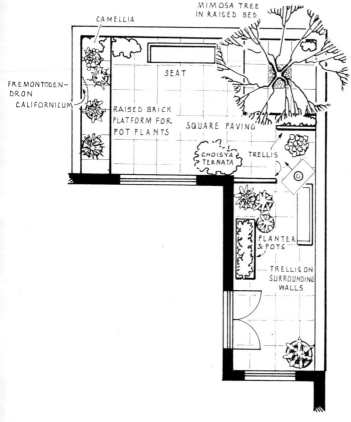

MIMOSA TREE IN RAISED BED

CAMELLIA

SEAT

FREMONTODEN-DRON CALIFORNICUM

RAISED BRICK PLATFORM FOR POT PLANTS

SQUARE PAVING

CHOISYA TERNATA

TRELLIS

PLANTER & POTS

TRELLIS ON SURROUNDING WALLS

(a plant usually associated with the greenhouse in this country) and a *Hibiscus syriacus* 'Blue Bird' complete the picture. Walking on past the first of the two teak benches in this garden, you are greeted by a shade-loving climbing hydrangea (*H. petiolaris*), and a fruiting outdoor grape (*Vitis vinifera* 'Brandt') which is happily growing up a trellis screen, sharing it with one of the three 'Madame Alfred Carrière' roses which run along the top of the wall. Immediately behind this screen, growing in a mulch of pebbles, is a delightful bamboo (*Arundinaria nitida*), and behind that, in the corner, a magnificent mimosa (*Acacia dealbata*) planted on a platform, again mulched with pebbles.

In the opposite corner stands a good-size *Camellia* 'Debutante' under which is growing a clump of *Euphorbia characias wulfenii*, as well as *Clematis* 'Lasurstern', with its roots well shaded from the sun. Against the house is growing Mexican orange blossom (*Choisya ternata*) on the one side, and a group of *Rosmarinus* 'Benenden Blue' on the other. Planted amongst the rosemary is a *Fremontodendron californicum* which laps up the afternoon sun and rewards its owner with showers of yellow, waxy, bell-shaped flowers for most of the summer. The *Wisteria sinensis* above the second teak bench exudes a scent which never fails to delight. Various other pots sit around the garden containing *Convolvulus mauritanicus*, *Fuchsia* 'Mrs Popple', *Hemerocallis* sp., *Hydrangea macrophylla* 'Lilacina' (in a huge Chinese pot) and, as if this is not enough, the garden explodes with the colour of succeeding pots of narcissi, tulips, lilies (*L. regale*), pinks and that more unusual form of busy lizzie with bronze-red leaves and vivid carmine flowers (*Impatiens petersiana*).

A tiny backyard made to seem very much larger as a result of clever and varying planting.

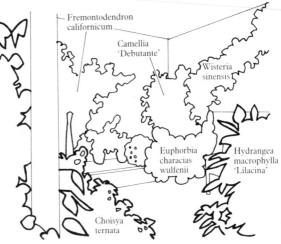

Fremontodendron californicum

Camellia 'Debutante'

Wisteria sinensis

Euphorbia characias wulfenii

Hydrangea macrophylla 'Lilacina'

Choisya ternata

A director's garden

LOCATION: *Pimlico*

This is a small west-facing garden. It is used as a *pied-à-terre* very occasionally during the year and therefore it has been planted to require very little maintenance. An ideal planting plan, therefore, for someone who is away a lot.

Here we see phormiums, hebes, ivies, *Euonymus* 'Emerald Gaiety', growing under the *Amelanchier canadensis*, as well as *Genista lydia*, Mexican orange blossom *(Choisya ternata)*, cotton lavender *(Santolina)* and *Fuchsia magellanica*. For colour during the summer, the pots are filled with pink, ivy-leaved pelargoniums (trailing 'geraniums').

The frog-down radiating brick paving always proves an effective way of treating a difficult, pointed corner such as this. It has been stepped in such a way as to 'push' the end of the garden backwards, so making the whole area seem larger than it really is. The brick and York paving, which covers the rest of the yard, blend very well together.

This is a minimum-maintenance garden planted with tough and compact plants. It belongs to a company whose directors make infrequent, short vists.

78

A retired couturier's garden

LOCATION: *South London*

This backyard has a distinctive tropical feel about it. Most of the potted plants spend the winter in a heated greenhouse, to be brought out into the garden for the summer. The rectangular water feature is half pond and half bog. The pond is planted with two water lilies (*Nymphaea* 'Paul Hariot' and 'Fire Crest'), with several fat gold fish to keep them company. The boggy section is planted up with 'Great Spearwort' (*Ranunculus lingua*), which grows between a mass of rounded pebbles. Under the magnificent *Gunnera manicata* by the pond is an ornamental grass, 'Gardener's Garters' (*Phalaris arundinacea* 'Picta').

The potted plants include a loquat (*Eriobotrya japonica*), two angel's trumpets (*Datura suaveolens*), two bananas (*Musa acuminata* 'Dwarf Cavendish' and *M. coccinea*), *Agave americana*, *Abutilon striatum* and *A. megapotamicum*, and a red passion flower (*Passiflora racemosa*), growing in the large 'Ali Baba' jar. Other plants include the ostrich fern (*Matteuccia struthiopteris*), *Aralia elata* 'Aureovariegata', *Hosta seiboldiana*, *Rheum palmatum* and *Fatsia japonica* 'Variegata'.

The owner of this garden was determined to introduce only exotic and 'out-of-scale' plants, and to 'get away from buttercups and daisies'. He has certainly succeeded in making it more interesting to the visitor!

Lush, 'tropical' planting can be achieved during the summer months in countries which have cold winters, so long as such tender plants can spend the winter in a heated greenhouse or conservatory. Although the majority of plants in this picture remain out of doors during the colder months a true tropical feeling is created when they are joined by banana, etc for the summer.

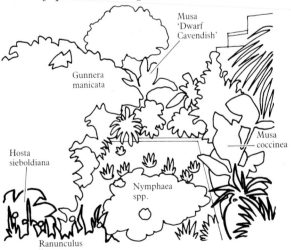

79

An art dealer's garden

OWNER: *Martin Summers Esq. of Chelsea*

What better treatment for a long, thin garden with very high walls either side? Here, the art of 'vertical' gardening must be mastered. Half-baskets attached to heavy-grade trellis smother the walls and the entire area has been tiled with terracotta squares. On the ground sit several pots containing camellias, hostas ferns, bergenias, climbing hydrangeas and *Actinidia chinensis*.

In order to ensure that this sunless area is always as colourful as possible, thought must be given as to the choice of plants which can best tolerate such shaded conditions, and still flower for long periods. In the spring and early summer, colour is supplied by primulas, primroses, which are then followed by fuchsias, trailing ivies and other bedding plants. Primulas play a very important part in this story, especially the species *P. malacoides* (the fairy primrose). They keep on flowering throughout the winter despite freezing temperatures.

The owner of this garden gives all the plants regular doses of Phostrogen, owing to the lack of light, and waters constantly during the summer.

Owner's gardening philosophy

'By using 14 in (35 cm) pots one can have more flexibility than in a normally planted garden. When trees and shrubs are in flower they can be put in the most visible place and lit at night. They can then be moved to another place when something else comes into flower. Walls must be used as surfaces to be covered by climbers and wall hanging pots, to create a vertical garden. As long as there is a lot of greenery, a few splashes of colour make it seem more colourful than it actually is.'

(Opposite) A very good example of 'vertical gardening'. There is little ground space so that full advantage of the wall space has been taken.

What better treatment for a roof garden? There are so many
containerized plants that the actual pots are scarcely visible.

7

FEATURES

The word 'feature' conjures up something special. A garden is often thought of as an extension or extra room to the house. I like that idea. There is no reason, therefore, why the garden shouldn't be treated as any other room in the house and slowly acquire ornaments and other miscellaneous *objets d'art*. A well-planned garden will include a focal point, i.e. a strategically placed fountain or other ornament, or indeed a very special plant. Such gardens automatically have a feature.

Colour plays a much more important part in interior decorating as it must remain pleasing and relaxing to the eye under artificial light. This is less of a problem with plants growing outside as Mother Nature's taste sees to it that the majority of plants, their leaves and flowers, are seldom objectionable. Sadly this is not always the case with modern hybrids. My particular hates are blue roses and green chrysanthemums, but then you, the reader, may love them and treat them as a feature!

Plants are very much more versatile than generally considered. Merely because *Garrya elliptica* is described as a wall shrub, why don't you plant one as a standard surrounded by lawn? Such plants are called 'wall shrubs' as they enjoy the protection of a wall, but if you have a sufficiently protected garden, there is no reason why you shouldn't plant them somewhere different. The hardy *Hibiscus (H. syriacus)* varieties can be trained as an 'umbrella' standard. The common bay, if kept regularly clipped throughout the summer, can take on the appearance of a magnificent slender evergreen pillar, and can grow as fast as three feet a year if all but the leading shoots are kept trimmed back.

Small gardens often contain one boring little tree which never does much. Instead of chopping it down, try growing a climbing rose up it, so making it a feature.

A little similar to topiary, there is a current fashion in America for ivy figures. Either grown in pots or out in the garden, ivy is encouraged to clothe whatever shape over chicken mesh or similar wire with a main framework of wire rods.

Paving needn't be plain paving. Leave a gap here and there for a small cushion plant, or a larger square mulched with gravel, through which spring and autumn bulbs can be encouraged to grow. Similarly, small supporting walls should always have gaps left in the brick or stone work for trailing and other plants.

Build an arbor over your garden bench and sit surrounded by scented plants as you admire the view. Turn your garden shed into a feature by attaching to it wings and a 'hat' made of trellis – the choice of gazebo or temple is enormous.

The longer a garden has been in your possession, the more bits and pieces you collect for it. A new terracotta pot here and a stone hedgehog peeping through a hosta there. Some people collect stamps. Why not collect winter-flowering plants and group them together in the small front garden? That would make a splendid feature.

(Far left) Every garden should contain a secret spot, hidden from the house by dense planting, where one can sit away from everything (and everybody).

(Left) A gap (in this case an arch) through a hedge or 'barrier' in a garden makes the visitor curious and compels him to probe further.

(Right) A delightful group of plants which complement each other, including border carnations, lavender, bay and *Euphorbia characias wulfenii*.

(Right) Many gardens have a corridor-like entrance to them. White-trellis supporting half and hanging baskets in front of a cream-coloured wall succeeds in turning a charmless area into an attractive one.

(Left) A bench enclosed by an arbor is an ideal place for relaxing. This bench is flanked by Mexican orange blossom (*Choisya ternata*) and surmounted by standard cotoneasters. A simple framework consisting of trellis and posts smothered in a scented climber is also very effective.

(Above) Interesting vegetative treatment for a border which gets very little sunlight. The plants include *Fatsia japonica*, *Garrya elliptica* and *Hedera colchica* 'Paddy's Pride'.

(Left) One of a series of specially made trellis pillars surrounding a garden. They supply 'instant height' and make ideal supports for less vigorous climbers.

(*Above*) This moorish formal garden was built in three weeks for the Chelsea Flower Show. The terracotta tiles and pots, as well as the plants succeed in further adding a warmer-climate feel to this backyard.

(*Right*) An interesting and, if necessary, mobile method of disguising a drain cover. Loose bricks have been arranged around the edge and pot placed in the middle. The gap has been infilled with compost and planted up with a selection of ivies. In an emergency, this could be disassembled without too much difficulty.

Recessed inspection covers are available on the market into which matching paving can be inserted.

(Above) Bare steps are enhanced with the addition of pots containing colourful flowers. These pink impatiens are an ideal choice as they flower the entire summer, having been preceded by *Tulipa* 'Apricot Beauty' in the spring.

(Left) Air vent painted to look like brickwork. Disguise ugly artefacts when possible.

APPENDIX I

PLANT LISTS

All plants included in these lists are usually commercially available.

A SELECTION OF PLANTS FOR SEMI-SHADE CONDITIONS

Trees

Acer palmatum (Japanese maple)   M
Eucalyptus gunnii (kept coppiced)   E, M
Hamamelis (witch hazel)   M
Ilex (holly)[1]   D, E
Taxus baccata (yew)   D, E, T

Shrubs

Arundinaria (bamboo; and other genera)   E, M, T
Azalea (many; deciduous)   M
Buxus sempervirens (box)   E, M
Camellia   E, T, W
Choisya ternata (Mexican orange blossom)   D, E
Cornus alba (dogwood; and other species)[1]   D
Cortaderia (pampas grass)   D, E
Cotoneaster (deciduous)   D
Euonymus (evergreen)   D

Euphorbia robbiae   E, M, T
Euphorbia characias wulfenii   E, M, T
Fatsia japonica[1]   E, M, T, W
Hippophae rhamnoides (sea buckthorn)[2]   D
Hydrangea   D
Mahonia   D, E, T, W
Pieris formosa forrestii[3]   E, M, T
Prunus laurocerasus (laurel)   D, E, T
Rhododendron (many)   E, M
Ribes (flowering currant)   D
Ruscus aculeatus (butcher's broom)   D, E, T
Sambucus nigra[4] (common elder)   D
Santolina (cotton lavender)   E, M
Skimmia japonica   D, E, T
Viburnum davidii (and other spp.)   D, E, T, W

Climbers and Wall shrubs

Chaenomoles speciosa (Japanese quince)   T
Clematis montana   M
Garrya elliptica[5]   E, T
Hedera (ivy)   D or M, T, W

---

1 Variegated species prefer more light.
2 Winter berries; must have male and female trees for berries.
3 Gives a better spring show if dappled sunlight filters through its red leaves.
4 *S. racemosa* 'Plumosa Aurea' (golden elder) needs more light.
5 Var. 'James Roof' has longer, more splendid catkins.

Key		M	Moist shade
A	Autumn tints	S	Slender upright growth
B	Winter berries	S/E	Semi-evergreen
Bk	Interesting bark	S/S	Tolerant of semi-shade
C	Spring catkins	T	Tolerant of total shade
D	Dry shade	Tw	Twisted or contorted branches
E	Evergreen	W	Winter flowering

Plants for semi-shade conditions *cont.*

Hydrangea petiolaris (climbing hydrangea)   D
   or M, T
Jasminum nudiflorum (winter jasmine)   D, T, W
Parthenocissus henryana   D or M
Parthenocissus quinquefolia (Virginia creeper)
   D or M
Pyracantha (winter berries)   D
Rosa[1]   M

Annuals

Aquilegia (hybrids; Columbine)   M
Cheiranthus (wall-flower)   D
Digitalis (foxglove; strictly speaking, a biennial)
   M
Lobelia (trailing lobelia)   M
Myosotis (forget-me-not)   D
Nicotiana (flowering tobacco)   M
Pelargonium (zonal 'geraniums')   M
Viola (pansy)   M

Ground Cover

Helleborus corsicus   M, T
Hypericum calycinum[2]   D, T
Lamiastrum galeobdolon   D, T
Lamium maculatum   D, T
Omphalodes cappadocica (creeping forget-me-
   not)   D, T
Pachysandra terminalis   D, T
Polygonatum   D, T
Pulmonaria   D, T

Sarcococca   D, T
Stachys   D, T
Symphoricarpos × *chenaultii* 'Hancock'   D, T
Vinca (periwinkle)   D, T
Ferns (many including *Adiantum* spp., *Osmunda
   regalis* and *Polystichum* spp.)   M, T

Herbaceous Perennials

Acanthus[3]   M
Arum   M, T
Asperula odorata (woodruff)   M, T
Bergenia cordifolia   D or M, T, W
Brunnera   D, T
Caltha (marsh marigold)   M, T
Carex (sedge)   M, T
Cimicifuga (bugbane)   M, T
Convallaria (lily of the valley)   D, T
Crocosmia masonorum   M, T
Dicentra (Dutchman's breeches)   M
Doronicum   D
Gaultheria procumbens (winter-green,
   checkerberry)   M, T
Geum   D
Gunnera[4]   M
Hemerocallis (day lily)   M, T
Heuchera (coral flower)   D, T
Hosta (plantain lily)   M, T
Iris foetidissima (the stinking iris)[5]   M, T
Ligularia   M, T
Liriope   D, T
Lobelia cardinalis   M
Meconopsis betonicifolia   M

---

1 'Danse de Feu', 'Goire de Dijon', 'Bobby James', 'Mermaid', 'Golden Showers' and others.
2 Winter berries.
3 Evergreen in milder area.
4 Best planted by water's edge.
5 Winter berries.

Key			
A	Autumn tints	M	Moist shade
B	Winter berries	S	Slender upright growth
Bk	Interesting bark	S/E	Semi-evergreen
C	Spring catkins	S/S	Tolerant of semi-shade
D	Dry shade	T	Tolerant of total shade
E	Evergreen	Tw	Twisted or contorted branches
		W	Winter flowering

Physalis (Chinese lantern)[1]   D
Polygonatum multiflorum (Solomon's seal)   D, T
Primula japonica (candelabra primulas)   M
Rodgersia   M, T
Smilacina (false Solomon's seal)   M, T
Thalictrum (meadow-rue)   D
Tradescantia × *andersoniana* (spiderwort)   M
Trollius (globe flower)   M, T

Bulbs and Corms
Crocus[2]
Cyclamen coum
Eranthis hyemalis (winter aconite)
Galanthus (snowdrop)[2]
Lilium martagon (stinking English lily; and others)
Muscari (grape hyacinth)
Narcissus (daffodils, narcissus)[2]

A SELECTION OF FAST-GROWING PLANTS FOR SCREENING

In many cases, the new owner of a garden is anxious to obliterate any ugly view as soon as possible. In the case of trees, it is always a good idea to plant another long-lived genus as close as possible, since fast-growing trees tend to have a shorter life-span. They all need open, sunny positions, unless otherwise indicated (S/S) in which case their growth is more sparse.

Trees
Acer (maple)[3]
Chamaecyparis lawsoniana (Lawson cypress)   E
× *Cupressocyparis leylandii*   E
Eucalyptus gunnii (eucalyptus; and other species)
Populus (poplar)
Robinia pseudoacacia (false acacia)
Salix (willow; especially planted as a stake)

Shrubs
Arundinaria (bamboo: especially *A. fastuosa*)   E, S/S
Ligustrum (privet)   S/E

Perennial Climbers
Clematis montana (varieties; also *C. tangutica*)   S/S
Humulus lupulus (hop)   S/S
Jasminum officinale (common white jasmine)
Lathyrus latifolius (perennial sweet pea)
Lonicera (honeysuckle)[4]
Passiflora caerulea (passion flower)
Polygonum baldschuanicum (Russian vine)[5]   S/S

Annual Climbers
Cobaea scandens (cup and saucer vine)[6]
Ipomoea (morning glory)
Lathyrus (sweet pea)
Runner beans

---

1 Produces more lanterns if given some sunshine.
2 Usually weaken in successive seasons if planted in total shade.
3 Especially *A. pseudoplatanus* (common sycamore).
4 Including *Lonicera japonica* 'Halliana', evergreen in mild winters.
5 The fastest!
6 May prove perennial in milder climates.

Key		M	Moist shade
A	Autumn tints	S	Slender upright growth
B	Winter berries	S/E	Semi-evergreen
Bk	Interesting bark	S/S	Tolerant of semi-shade
C	Spring catkins	T	Tolerant of total shade
D	Dry shade	Tw	Twisted or contorted branches
E	Evergreen	W	Winter flowering

A SELECTION OF PLANTS WITH SCENTED FLOWERS

Trees

Acacia dealbata (in milder areas)   W
Hamamelis mollis (witch hazel; also *H. vernalis*)   W, S/S
Laurus nobilis (bay)   S/S
Magnolia (many)
Malus (many)
Myrtus apiculata (myrtle)
Prunus (many)
Rhododendron edgeworthii (hybrids; tree rhododendron)
Rhododendron maddenii (hydrids; tree rhododendron)
Tilia oliveri (lime)[1]

Shrubs

Berberis (many)
Buddleia (many)   S/S
Choisya ternata (Mexican orange blossom)   W, S/S
Corylopsis pauciflora
Daphne bholua 'Gurkha'   S/S
Daphne mezereum   S/S
Daphne odora   W, S/S
Erica (many)   W
Lavandula (lavender)
Mahonia japonica   W, S/S
Philadelphus
Pittosporum
Rhododendron (many)   S/S
Ribes (many)   S/S

Rosa (many)[2]   S/S
Sambucus (elder)
Sarcococca (all)   W, S/S
Syringa (lilac)
Viburnum (many)[3]   W, S/S

Climbers

Actinidia chinensis (Chinese gooseberry)[4]   S/S
Ceanothus (many)
Chimonanthus praecox (winter sweet)   W, S/S
Clematis armandii
Clematis cirrhosa balearica   S/S
Clematic flammula (virgin's bower)[5]
Cytisus battandieri
Jasminum (jasmine; many)   S/S
Lonicera fragrantissima (winter-flowering honeysuckle; many)   S/S
Rosa (many)
Trachelospermum jasminoides
Wisteria (all)

Annuals

Centaurea moschata (sweet sultan)
Cheiranthus (wall flower)   S/S
Dianthus barbatus (sweet william)
Hesperis matronalis (sweet rocket)
Lathyrus odoratus (sweet pea)
Matthiola (stock)
Nicotiana (flowering tobacco)   S/S

Herbaceous Perennials

Bergenia schmidtii   S/S
Convallaria (lily of the valley)   S/S
Eremerus spp. (foxtail lily)

---

1 Does not drip or sucker.
2 Especially 'old-fashioned' varieties.
3 Some are winter flowering, including *V. tinus*.
4 West wall.
5 Fragrant.

Key				
A	Autumn tints	M	Moist shade
B	Winter berries	S	Slender upright growth
Bk	Interesting bark	S/E	Semi-evergreen
C	Spring catkins	S/S	Tolerant of semi-shade
D	Dry shade	T	Tolerant of total shade
E	Evergreen	Tw	Twisted or contorted branches
		W	Winter flowering

A SELECTION OF PLANTS WITH ALL-YEAR-ROUND INTEREST

Trees and Shrubs

Acacia dealbata (mimosa)[1]
Acer davidii   A, Bk
Acer griseum   A, Bk
Acer pensylvanicum   A, Bk
Acer rufinerve   A, Bk
Arundinaria (bamboo; and other bamboo genera)
   E
Aucuba japonica (spotted laurel)[2]   B, E
Betula pendula (silver birch)   Bk
Camellia[3]   E
Cortaderia (pampas grass)[4]   E
Coryllus avellana 'Contorta' *(corkscrew hazel)*
   C, Tw
Cryptomeria japonica   A, E
Phormium tenax (New Zealand flax)[5]   E
Prunus 'Otto Luyken'   E
Rosa moyesii   A, B, Bk
Salix matsudana 'Tortuosa' (dragon's claw
   willow)[6]   A, Tw
Taxodium distichum (swamp cypress)[7]   A
Viburnum × bodnantense   E, W

A SELECTION OF MEDIUM-SIZED TREES FOR THE SMALLER BACKYARD

Acer drummondii
Acer griseum (paper bark maple)

Acer palmatum (Japanese maple)[8]
Acer pseudoplatanus 'Brilliantissimum'
Alnus glutinosa 'Aurea'
Arbutus unedo (strawberry tree)
Betula pendula (weeping silver birch)
Carpinus betulus 'Columnaris'   S
Cercis siliquastrum (judas tree)
Eriobotrya japonica (loquat)[9]
Ficus (fig)[10]
Fothergilla monticola
Gleditsia triacanthos 'Sunburst' (and other
   varieties)
Juniperus virginiana 'Sky Rocket'   S
Laburnum watereri 'Vossii'[11]
Laurus nobilis (bay)[12]   S
Magnolia stellata[13]
Morus nigra (black mulberry)[14]
Parrotia persica
Prunus 'Amanogawa' (short-lived)   S
Prunus subhirtella 'Autumnalis' (winter-
   flowering cherry)
Prunus subhirtella 'Fukubana'   S
Rhus typhina (stag's horn sumach)[15]
Robinia pseudoacacia 'Frisia'[16]
Sorbus 'Joseph Rock'
Sorbus aucuparia
Syringa (lilac)
Trachycarpus fortunei (windmill or Chusan
   palm)[17]

---

1 For warmer climates only.
2 The author detests it; however, it is very useful for filtering noise and dirt and for screening a barbeque.
3 Shiny leaves throughout the winter, never plant against an east-facing wall otherwise frozen flowers become browned off
   when the warm rays of the sun hit them.
4 Especially 'Sunningdale Silver' which retains its plumes throughout the winter in milder areas.
5 Sword-like leaves.
6 Holds on to its leaves well into the winter.
7 Sends 'knees' up from the water if planted at water's edge.
8 Highly recommended.
9 For milder areas only.
10 'Brown Turkey' is a prolific fruiter; all varieties must have their roots restricted.
11 Produces fewer poisonous seed pods.
12 Can be clipped as a pillar or lolly pop.
13 One of first to flower in spring, producing blooms on the bare branches.
14 Can become large eventually.
15 Especially 'Laciniata' which has a more interesting, finely cut leaf.
16 Can become large eventually.
17 One of the toughest and most frost resistant of palms.

APPENDIX II
THE BEAUTIFUL BACKYARD—
THE D.I.Y. WAY

Do's

1 Try to live with your newly inherited garden for one season, if practicable. You will thus be able to 'learn to live with it' as well as avoiding rushed decisions and be able to decide on which plants you want to keep. Read nursery catalogues!

2 Decide on the function of the garden. Are there children? If so, you will need a swing, sand pit and Wendy House. Do you want to use it for meditation and escape from the world outside? If so, you will need thick and lush planting.

3 Are there eye-sores or neighbours' windows you wish to screen? This will decide on the positioning of trees or trellis.

4 Decide on which windows are going to be used the most. These must command the best views and the positioning of the focal point.

5 Take a survey of the garden and submit it to paper to scale. On the plan clearly show which direction the garden faces and the spread of existing trees. This will decide on your choice of plants for shaded and difficult areas. (See plant lists, p. 89).

6 Take a soil sample. If the pH of your soil is alkaline you will not be able to grow rhododendrons. If it is very acid your brassica crops will not come to much.

7 Mark it out with pegs and white string to see if it works out on site.

8 First build 'hard landscape' features such as patios, trellis, paving,* etc. Depending on how long this is going to take, plan it so that it is finished during the autumn, then planting can take place in early winter (with later additions in the spring if necessary).

9 Prepare the ground, incorporating generous amounts of well-rotted organic matter, ideally down to the depth of two spits of a spade.

10 Plant and mulch.

Don'ts

1 Never expect to have an 'instant' garden in the U.K. You will have to wait at least five years to allow plants to mature. It always proves to be a mistake to be in too much of a rush to get things going. Fast-growing plants often become too invasive later on.

2 Never plant shrubs, and especially trees, too close together, despite the fact that the garden may look too empty to start off with.

3 Never chop down or shape an existing mature tree without first finding out if it is protected (with a Tree Preservation Order). To avoid a steep fine, check with your local Council first.

4 Never establish a lawn in too small a space. They are of course lovely for children, but their upkeep is difficult and they will always look messy.

5 Avoid planting too many high-maintenance plants. Sadly, roses fall into this category. Cut down on herbaceous perennials and other plants which require mulching, feeding, staking, pruning, dead-heading, etc.

---

* Always make sure that paving near to the house slopes slightly away from it.

INDEX

See also Appendix I (pp. 89–93) for further citation of plant names

Abutilon megapotamicum, 32, 79; *striatum*, 79

Acacia dealbata, 76

Acanthus mollis, 12, 41; *spinosus*, 36, 56

Acer macrophyllum, 19; *palmatum*, 37; *pseudoplatanus*, 13, 17, 22; *velutinum vanvolxemii*, 20

Actinidia chinensis, 19, 80; *kolomikta*, 19, 43

Agapanthus, 40; *umbellatus*, 12

Agave americana, 79

Ajuga reptans 'Burgundy Glow', 67

Akebia quinata, 36, 54

Alchemilla mollis, 12, 40

Allium triquetrum, 18, 22

Amelanchier canadensis, 78; *lamarckii*, 37

Aponogeton distachyus, 12

Aralia elata 'Aureovariegata', 19, 79

Aristolochia macrophylla, 19, 36, 45

Artemisia arborescens, 72; 'Lambrook Silver', 37

Arundinaria fastuosa, 17; *japonica*, 15, 20; *murieliae*, 15, 22, 64; *nitida*, 17, 36, 56, 76; *viridistriata*, 19, 37

Asperula odorata, 22, 36

Asplenium scolopendrium, 20, 36

Athyrium filix-femina, 20

Aucuba japonica, 41

Azalea, 30, 41

Begonia, fibrous, 30, 72

Bergenia, 80; 'Ballawley', 41; *cordifolia*, 33

Betula pendula, 20, 24

Blackberry, 52; hybrid, 43

Bluebell, 15

Bracken, 22

Buddleia 'Lochinch', 76

Bupleurum falcatum, 18

Buxus sempervirens, 64

Camellia, 26, 30, 45, 46, 50, 64, 70, 80; *japonica*

'Adolphe Audusson', 15; 'Apollo', 17; 'Bow Bells', 66; 'C. F. Coates', 17; 'Contessa Lavinia Maggi', 10; 'Debutante', 76; 'Golden Spangles', 66; 'Guilio Nuccio', 12; Lady Clare, 66; 'Tricolor', 66; × *williamsii* 'Donation', 12, 33, 66; 'Francis Hanger', 12; 'Mary Christian, 50

Campanula, 12

Carex pendula, 18, 43

Catalpa bignonioides, 19 × *erubescens*, 20

Ceanothus 'Burkwoodii', 12

Ceratostigma willmottianum, 12

Cercidiphyllum japonicum, 19

Cercis siliquastrum, 17

Chamaecyparis lawsoniana, 20

Cherry, 12, 20, 62

Chimonanthus praecox, 32

Choisya ternata, 17, 33, 40, 45, 76, 78

Chrysanthemum 'White Bonnet', 12

Cistus, 39

Clematis, 72; 'Etoile Violette', 12; × *jackmanii*, 13, 32, 42; × *jouiniana*, 45; 'Lasurstern', 76; 'Miss Bateman', 12; *montana*, 36, 45; 'Nelly Moser', 32; 'Rouge Cardinal', 12

Cobaea scandens, 36

Conifers, 72

Convallaria, 15

Convolvulus cneorum, 76; *mauritanicus*, 76; *tricolor*, 43

Cordyline, 30; *australis*, 36, 46

Cornus, 39, 70; *alba*, 89; 'Sibirica', 15; 'Spaethii', 56

Corylus maxima 'Purpurea', 19

Cotinus coggygria, 40

Cotoneaster, 89; *horizontalis*, 33, 39

Crab apple, 45

Crocosmia masonorum, 42, 43

Cryptomeria japonica 'Elegans', 19, 56

Cytisus battandieri, 32; × *kewensis*, 76

Daphne odora, 40

Datura suaveolens, 79

Dianthus, 40

Dicentra 'Langtrees', 12

Dicksonia antarctica, 20

Digitalis, 15, 36, 42

Dipladenia, 74

Dryopteris pseudomas, 36, 67

Elaeagnus pungens 'Maculata', 17, 39, 40

Erica arborea, 12

Erigeron macranthus, 12

Eriobotrya japonica, 36, 79

Escallonia macrantha, 40

Eucalyptus, 64; *niphophila*, 45

Euonymus, 39; 'Emerald Gaiety', 78

Euphorbia characias wulfenii, 36, 40, 42, 76; *robbiae*, 17

Fagus sylvatica 'Roseomarginata', 19

Fatsia japonica, 17, 19, 37, 45, 50, 62; 'Variegata', 19, 79

Fig, 26

Foxglove, 15, 36, 42

Fremontodendron californicum, 32, 63, 76

Fuchsia, 12, 72, 80; *magellanica*, 78; 'Versicolor', 36; 'Mrs Popple', 76

Garrya elliptica, 22, 32, 83, 'James Roof', 42

Gazania × *hybrida* 'Bridget', 43

Genista hispanica, 16; *lydia*, 78

Geranium 'Johnson's Blue', 37; *macrorrhizum*, 22; *phaeum*, 12

Ginkgo biloba, 13

Gleditsia, 39

Griselina littoralis, 46

Gunnera manicata, 12, 18, 20, 79

Hebe, 40, 78; 'Blue Clouds', 12

Hedera canariensis, 50; 'Variegata', 41; *colchica* 'Paddy's Pride', 76, 86; *helix*, 52; 'Buttercup', 66; 'Discolor', 17; 'Goldheart', 15, 66; 'Sagittifolia', 66

Hedychium gardnerianum, 20

Helianthemum, 12, 40

Helleborus foetidus, 15; *niger*, 70; *orientalis*, 36; *sternii*, 36

Helxine, 70

Hemerocallis, 76

Heuchera 'Greenfinch', 22

Hibiscus syriacus, 83; 'Blue Bird', 76; 'Coelestis', 17

Honeysuckle, 12, 13

Hosta, 33; *elata*, 70; *fortunei* 'Albopicta', 36, 67; 'Aureo-marginata', 15; *plantaginea*, 70; *sieboldiana*, 15, 42, 56, 79; 'Elegans', 20; 'Thomas Hogg', 15, 36, 42, 56

Humulus lupulus 'Aureus', 52

Hydrangea, 39, 40, 70; *macrophylla* 'Lilacina', 76; *petiolaris*, 32, 42, 58, 70, 76, 80; *sargentiana*, 20; *villosa*, 36

Ilex aquifolium 'J. C. van Tol', 36

Impatiens, 30, 72; *petersiana*, 76

Iris, bearded, 67; 'Desert Song', 15; *foetidissima*, 22, 56

Jasminum officinale, 15, 32, 52; *polyanthum*, 74

Laburnum, 15

Lamiastrum galeobdolon, 17

Lapageria rosea, 74

Laurus nobilis, 17, 40
Lavandula 'Hidcote', 37, 40, 43
Liatris callilepis, 43
Ligularia dentata 'Desdemona', 10, 20; hessei, 20; veitchiana, 20; wilsoniana, 20
Ligustrum lucidum, 17; ovalifolium 'Aureum', 17
Lilium, 12; regale, 76
Lonicera × americana, 32; fragrantissima, 12
Lunaria, 74
Lupin, 43
Lysichitum, 20; americanum, 10; hybrid, 12

Macleaya, 15
Magnolia delavayi, 19; evergreen, 26; grandiflora, 50; 'Exmouth', 12, 13; wilsonii, 46
Mahonia, 46; bealei, 12, 16; 'Charity', 40
Matteuccia struthiopteris, 79
Mentha pulegium, 67
Minuartia, 56
Mirrors, 49–50
Miscanthus sinensis 'Gracillimus', 56
Morus nigra, 15, 46
Muehlenbeckia complexa, 22
Murals, 49
Musa acuminata 'Dwarf Cavendish', 79; basjoo, 20; coccinea, 79

Nephrolepis exaltata, 70
Nerine bowdenii, 12
Nicotiana, 15, 30
Nymphaea alba 'Minor', 37; 'Fire Crest', 79; 'Paul Hariot', 79

Olearia, 39; × haastii, 50
Olive tree, 17

Onoclea sensibilis, 10, 70
Osmunda regalis, 10, 20; 'Purpurascens', 20

Pachysandra terminalis 'Variegata', 22
Paeonia 'Sarah Bernhardt', 15
Papaver somniferum, 15
Parrotia persica, 20
Parthenocissus henryana, 42, 52, 58; quinquefolia, 32
Passiflora caerulea, 15, 33; racemosa, 79
Paulownia tomentosa, 20
Peach, 45
Pelargonium, ivy-leaved, 78; zonal, 30
Peltiphyllum peltatum, 20
Petasites fragrans, 18; hybridus, 20
Petunia, 30
Phalaris arundinacea 'Picta', 79
Philadelphus 'Sybille', 36
Phormium, 46, 78; tenax, 15, 19; 'Purpureum', 33, 37; 'Variegatum', 50
Pieris formosa forrestii, 39, 40, 89; 'Wakehurst', 42; japonica 'Variegata', 39
Piptanthus laburnifolius, 40
Pittosporum, 39; tobira, 74
Platycerium bifurcatum, 70
Plumbago, 74
Polygonatum × hybridum, 36
Polygonum baldschuanicum, 70; sachalinense, 20; 'Variegatum', 20
Polypodium vulgare, 22
Polystichum setiferum 'Densum', 36, 56, 70; 'Divisilobum', 20
Populus lasiocarpa, 19
Potentilla fruticosa 'Abbotswood', 37
Primula bulleyana, 67; malacoides, 80

Prunus laurocerasus, 89; subhirtella 'Autumnalis', 66; 'A. Rosea', 12; 'Tai Haku', 20
Pyracantha, 90

Ranunculus lingua, 79
Rheum palmatum, 12, 36, 79
Rhododendron, 13, 56, 39, 46, 50, 'President Roosevelt', 62; sinogrande, 19; yakushimanum, 12, 62, 70
Rhus typhina, 24
Robinia pseudoacacia, 22; 'Frisia', 12, 24, 46
Rodgersia podophylla, 20; tabularis, 20
Roses (Rosa), 72; 'Bloomfield Abundance', 12; 'Bobbie James', 12; 'Copenhagen', 62; 'Danse de Feu', 32; 'Emily Grey', 32; 'Ena Harkness', 15; 'Etoile de Hollande', 12; 'Frühlingsgold', 12; 'Gloire de Dijon', 32; 'Golden Showers', 43; 'Iceberg', 12; 'Kiftsgate', 45; 'Little White Pet', 12; 'Louise Odier', 12; 'Madame Alfred Carrière', 36, 76; 'Madame Gregoire Staechelin', 56; 'Mermaid', 32, 62; 'Mousseline', 12; 'New Dawn', 62; 'Peace', 62; 'Penelope', 12; 'Perle d'Or', 12; 'Plentiful', 12;
Rosmarinus officinalis, 33, 43; 'Benenden Blue', 76
Rudbeckia fulgida, 43

Salvia nemorosa 'Superba', 37; officinalis 'Purpurascens', 76
Sambucus racemosa 'Plumosa Aurea', 20, 36
Santolina, 42, 78; neopolitanum, 76

Sasa palmata, 20
Saxifraga 'Cloth of Gold', 6
Schizostylis coccinea, 40
Scrophularia vernalis, 18
Sedum, 12
Selinum tenuifolium, 36
Senecio greyi, 39; 'Sunshine', 40
Smyrnium perfoliatum, 18
Snowdrops, 70
Solanum, 36

Taxus baccata 'Fastigiata Aureomarginata', 62
Tellima grandiflora 'Purpurea', 41
Teucrium fruticans, 12
Thalictrum dipterocarpum, 4
Thyme, 76
Tiarella cordifolia, 33
Trachelospermum jasminoide 36
Trachystemon orientale, 12, 2
Trachycarpus fortunei, 15, 2 39, 50
Tradescantia × andersoniana 'Flore Pleno', 43
Trifolium repens 'Purpurea', 67
Typha minima, 37

Ulmus camperdownii, 24

Viburnum davidii, 12, 20; rhytidophyllum, 19
Vinca, 22; minor, 15, 50
Viola, 12
Vitis, 26, 52; coignetiae, 36; vinifera, 45; 'Brandt', 42, 76

Weigela, 39, 40
Wisteria sinensis, 15, 26, 50, 76; 'Alba', 32, 43

Yucca gloriosa, 13

Zantedeschia aethiopica, 19